Petersburg National Battlefield and Richmond National Battlefield Park

Weather of 2007

Natural Resource Data Series NPS/MIDN/NRDS—2010/051

Paul Knight, Tiffany Wisniewski, Chad Bahrmann, and Sonya Miller

Pennsylvania State Climate Office
503 Walker Building
Pennsylvania State University
University Park, Pennsylvania 16802

May 2010

U.S. Department of the Interior
National Park Service
Natural Resource Program Center
Fort Collins, Colorado

The National Park Service, Natural Resource Program Center publishes a range of reports that address natural resource topics of interest and applicability to a broad audience in the National Park Service and others in natural resource management, including scientists, conservation and environmental constituencies, and the public.

The Natural Resource Data Series is intended for timely release of basic data sets and data summaries. Care has been taken to assure accuracy of raw data values, but a thorough analysis and interpretation of the data has not been completed. Consequently, the initial analyses of data in this report are provisional and subject to change.

All manuscripts in the series receive the appropriate level of peer review to ensure that the information is scientifically credible, technically accurate, appropriately written for the intended audience, and designed and published in a professional manner. This report received informal peer review by subject-matter experts who were not directly involved in the collection, analysis, or reporting of the data. Data in this report were collected and analyzed using methods based on established, peer-reviewed protocols and were analyzed and interpreted within the guidelines of the protocols.

Views, statements, findings, conclusions, recommendations, and data in this report are those of the author(s) and do not necessarily reflect views and policies of the National Park Service, U.S. Department of the Interior. Mention of trade names or commercial products does not constitute endorsement or recommendation for use by the National Park Service.

This report is available from the Mid-Atlantic Network (http://science.nature.nps.gov/im/units/MIDN) and the Natural Resource Publications Management website (http://www.nature.nps.gov/publications/NRPM).

Please cite this publication as:

NPS 325/102304, 367/102304, May 2010

Contents

Figures

Tables

List of Key Acronyms

COOP	National Weather Service Cooperative Observer Program
CWOP	Citizen Weather Observer Program
FAA	Federal Aviation Administration
IFLOWS	Integrated Flood Observing and Warning System
NADP	National Atmospheric Deposition Program
NARR	North American Regional Reanalysis
NB	National Battlefield
NBP	National Battlefield Park
NCDC	National Climatic Data Center
NWS	National Weather Service
PDSI	Palmer Drought Severity Index
PETE	Petersburg National Battlefield
PRISM	Parameter-elevation Regressions on Independent Slopes Model
RAWS	Remote Automated Weather Stations
RICH	Richmond National Battlefield Park
USGS	United States Geological Survey

Purpose of the Report

Weather and climate are widely recognized as key drivers of terrestrial and aquatic ecosystems, affecting biotic as well as abiotic ecosystem characteristics and processes. Global and regional scale climatic patterns, trends, and variations are critical to the cycling of elements, nutrients, and minerals through the ecosystems and can deliver pollutants from regional and even global sources. These variations and trends influence the fundamental properties of ecologic systems such as soil-water relationships and plant-soil processes and their disturbance rates and intensity. Information obtained from meteorological monitoring will be useful to interpreting and understanding changes in species composition, community structure, water and soil chemistry, and related landscape processes.

The purpose of this report is to provide a concise climate summary for January 1 to December 31, 2007, and to place current patterns and trends in an appropriate historical, regional, and global context (Knight et all, in preparation). It is our intention that this report will satisfy an inherent interest in meteorological phenomena, meet the Mid-Atlantic Network (MIDN) Weather and Climate Monitoring objectives:

- Document long-term trends in weather and climate through seasonal and annual summaries of selected parameters (e.g., multiple forms of precipitation, temperature).
- Identify and document extremes and averages of climatic conditions for common parameters (e.g., precipitation, air temperature), and other parameters where sufficient data are available (e.g., wind speed and direction, solar radiation).
- Provide information on near real-time weather parameters, historical climate patterns, and climate station metadata from a single, easy to use Internet portal.

To accomplish these objectives, a variety of atmospheric data streams were evaluated for their quality, longevity, and applicability to the MIDN parks. Since no single weather observing network contains all the pertinent measures of atmospheric phenomena to assess ecosystem health, an objective analysis of the data networks was developed. Through this analysis, a select number of stations were chosen as representative of each park and these are the primary data sources used in the profile of last year's climate summary and trends.

Weather Summary

Overall, 2007 was warmer and drier than the long-term average. While the calendar year began quite mild, the period from mid-January until late-February was consistently cold with a couple snow and ice events. March turned milder with near average rainfall. Another bout of rather cold air was noted in April that lasted until mid-month with a departure of 1–3°F (0.6–1.8°C) from normal maximum temperature for April. A widespread rainstorm occurred on April 15th with some sections receiving more than 2.3 in (58 mm) in one day. Rain became lighter and infrequent during May, but June saw regular showers and warmer than average temperatures. July was cooler and drier than normal. The hottest weather of the summer came in early August. Very warm weather in September continued into much of October with departures of 5–7°F (3–4°C) for maximum temperature in October. November was cool and quite dry and the year concluded with mild air. Both snowfall and rainfall for 2007 were noticeably below average (Table 1).

Long-term Trends

The rise in winter minimum temperatures continued in 2007. However, the lengthening of the growing season showed little change in 2007. The occurrence of the 'last' frost (mid-April) and a late first freeze (late October) made this year near normal in length. The trend toward milder winter nights continued in 2007 despite a late January to mid-February cold snap which produced single readings on a couple of (-14°C) mornings (Table 1). While summer (Jul–Aug–Sep) was the wettest period in 2007 it was not as wet as previous summers and only a bit above normal.

The factors that influence seasonal trends are ocean temperature anomalies. The longer-term effects of a change in water temperatures to lower (cool) values around the rim of the North Pacific adjacent to North America are impacting autumn temperatures (warmer than usual Sept–Oct) as well as the frequency of cold air outbreaks during the winter in Virginia (more often). A minimum in solar activity (very few sunspots), which often correlates to slowly dropping mean annual temperatures, was also noted in 2007.

Table 1. Summary of 2007 significant weather indicators for Petersburg NB and Richmond NBP.

Weather Indicators	2007 Statistics	Comments on Trends
Hot Days (days with Tmax ≥ 90°F/32°C)	49–53	Above the 30-year mean of 41
Cold Days (days with Tmax ≤ 32°F/0°C)	0–2	Below the 30-year mean of 7
Winter Minimums (lowest temperature)	~7°F -14°C	Below the long term average of -3°F (-18°C)
Growing Season Length (days between last 32°F/0°C in spring and first 32°F/0°C in fall)	191–212	Near the 30-year mean of 200–210
Annual Precipitation	25–41 in 635–1041 mm	Below the average of 44 in (1118 mm)
Annual Snowfall	1–5 in 3–13 cm	Below the 30-year mean of 12 in (305 mm)

The Climate of the Greater Richmond Area

The Southeast section of Virginia is generally considered to have a humid continental type of climate with relatively flat terrain keeping conditions homogeneous (Davey et al. 2006). The prevailing westerly winds carry most of the weather disturbances that affect the region from the interior of the continent, so that the Atlantic Ocean has occasional influence on the climate of the area. Coastal storms do, at times, affect the day-to-day weather, especially in the winter. Also, storms of tropical origin can have significant effect within this part of Virginia, causing severe floods in some instances.

Temperatures are moderately continental with the tempering effects due to the nearby ocean that contributes to cloud production in the summer and onshore winds modifying the chill at times during the winter. The lowest readings in the winter occur with polar air masses of Canadian origin settling over the Northeast after a fresh snowfall. The highest readings of the summer happen when the sub-tropical fair weather system, the Bermuda high, pushes westward into the Carolinas. Its clockwise circulation will direct hot, humid air from the Gulf region into the area. The southwest winds gain additional warmth when descending the Appalachians. The last freeze typically occurs in early April and the first frosts appear in November.

Precipitation is fairly evenly distributed throughout the year. Annual amounts generally range between 40 to 48 in (1016–1219 mm), while the majority of the area receives about 44 in (1118 mm). Greatest amounts usually occur in the late spring and summer months, while February is the driest month, having about 2 in (50.8mm) less than the wettest months. Precipitation tends to be somewhat greater at the coast, due primarily to coastal storms which occasionally frequent the area. During the warm season these storms can bring heavy rain, while in winter, heavy snow or a mixture of rain and snow may be produced.

Surface winds blow from the west and northwest in the cold season and from the southwest during the warm half of the year. Thunderstorms follow a frequency that matches the solar cycle, occurring between the equinoxes and reaching a peak near the solstice. Hail is relatively infrequent, occurring about once every other year, but flash floods and damaging thunderstorm winds affect parts of the parks each summer. On average, tornadoes pass through the area about once every three years. The direct effects of an Atlantic hurricane are infrequent, though remnant rains from tropical storms have contributed to the region's worst floods.

Observing Stations

In addition to the summary information available in this report, a Web interface is available that has a variety of data sources in near real-time (Figure 1). Select NPS Inventory and Monitoring Network in upper right corner and then directly below this, choose a network. You can also filter weather monitoring stations by various categories. We encourage you to take a few minutes to go through the tutorial that describes the attributes of this site: http://climate.met.psu.edu/gmaps/NPS_DEVELOPMENT/NPStutorial.2.26.08.pdf.

A total of 32 weather observing stations comprising five weather observing networks were selected around Petersburg NB and Richmond NBP (Table 2). The station identifiers in blue text (Figure 2) indicate those from which data has been used within this report. Stations that are not in the blue or bold text contain incomplete data for 2007 (Table 3).

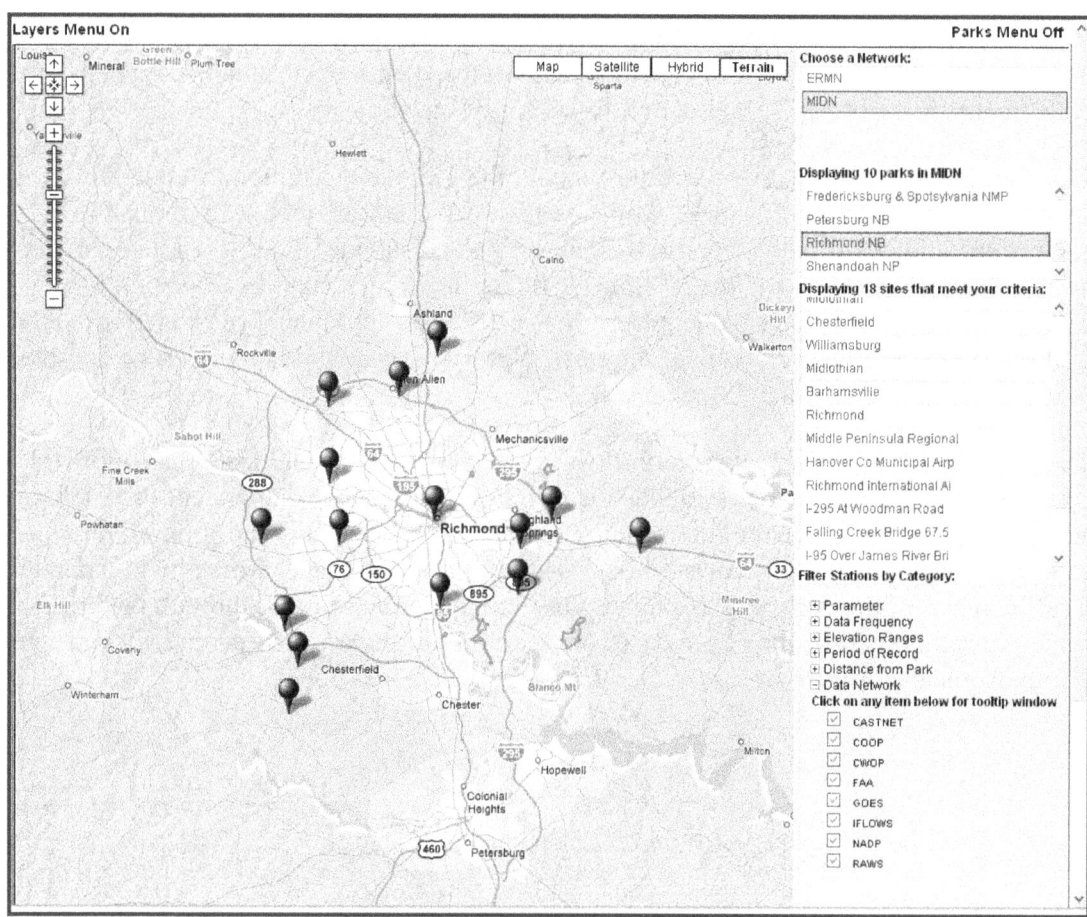

Figure 1. A snapshot of the Web interface that is available at http://climate.met.psu.edu/gmaps/NPS_DEVELOPMENT/interface.php/.

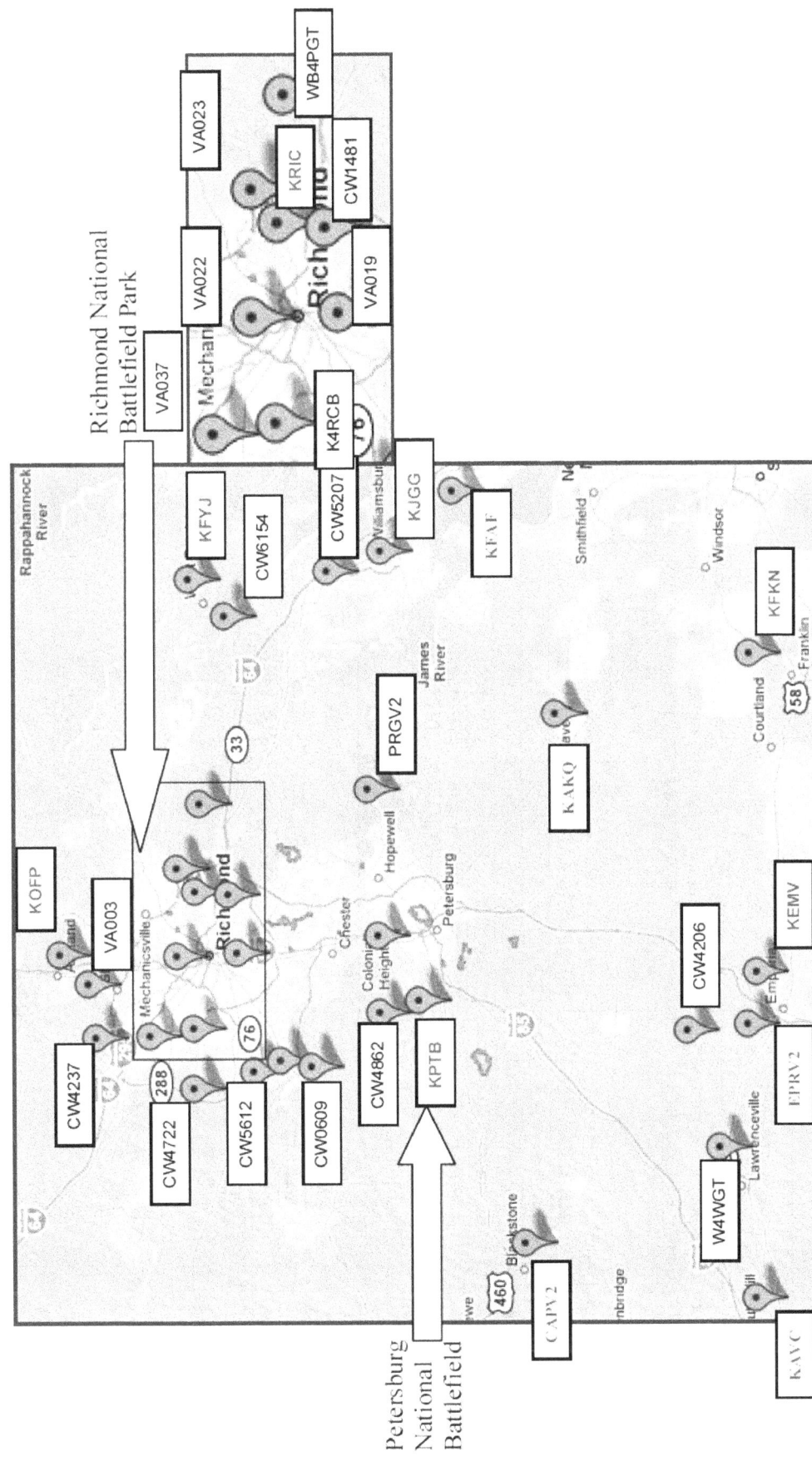

Figure 2. Location of weather observing stations around Petersburg NB and Richmond NBP.

Table 2. Listing of the five data networks around Petersburg NB and Richmond NBP.

Data Network	Number of Stations
CWOP	13
FAA	10
VADOT	6
COOP	2
RAWS	1

Table 3. List of weather observing stations around Petersburg NB and Richmond NBP. Those that are in bold have been selected as representative of the park in large part due to the percent time of reporting during 2007. Not all data networks are shown here – missing are: CWOP, VADOT and RAWS because their data are either incomplete or not quality assured.

Station	Observing Network	Station Name	Period of Record (POR)		Percentage of Time Reporting Temperature for 2007	Percentage of Time Reporting Precipitation for 2007	Percentage of Time Reporting Temperature for entire POR	Percentage of Time Reporting Precipitation for entire POR
KFYJ	FAA	Middle Peninsula	2004-01-01	Present	**97.8**	0.0	91.3	11.1
KOFP	FAA	Hanover	1996-01-01	Present	**97.3**	**97.3**	93.3	93.6
KRIC	FAA	Richmond	1949-02-01	Present	**100.0**	**100.0**	95.8	95.8
KAKQ	FAA	Wakefield	1997-01-01	Present	**100.0**	**100.0**	96.5	95.9
KAVC	FAA	Mecklenburg	1997-01-01	Present	**99.2**	**99.2**	95.1	85.1
KEMV	FAA	Emporia	2002-02-28	Present	40.5	40.5	30.0	8.2
KFAF	FAA	Felker Army Airfield	1996-01-02	Present	**88.8**	0.0	71.4	8.3
KFKN	FAA	Franklin	1996-01-01	Present	**97.8**	0.0	94.6	9.6
KJGG	FAA	Williamsburg	2003-01-01	Present	**99.2**	**99.2**	94.0	89.9
KPTB	FAA	Petersburg	1996-01-01	Present	**95.6**	**95.6**	75.9	75.9
CAPV2	COOP	Camp Pickett	1972-08-01	Present	**100.0**	**99.5**	98.0	98.0
EPRV2	COOP	Emporia	1920-01-01	Present	**100.0**	**100.0**	29.4	84.6

6

Temperature Summary

The year began quite mild, but it turned much colder in mid-January. The period from January 17–February 20 featured numerous sub-freezing nights and a couple of sub-freezing days. It was during this time that a bit of snow fell. The winter's most widespread snow and ice came around Valentine's Day when between 0.5–2 in (1–5 cm) of snow fell across the region. The snow was mixed with sleet and freezing rain in many sections. March turned milder and was a bit wetter (Table 4). A ten-day period of unseasonably cold weather was accompanied by late hard freezes in the first half of April. The cold snap ended with a powerful nor'easter bringing widespread heavy rainfall on April 15. The month of May turned warmer and the regular rains ended as it turned quite dry (Tables 5, 6, and 7).

The summer of 2007 had several episodes of hot weather with warm season daily departures >+5°F (+2.8°C) from May 25–June 3, August 1–10 (the hottest spell), and September 4–11. Oddly, the most anomalously warm weather did not occur until October 4–10 when readings averaged more than +10°F (5.6°C) above the long-term mean for this week-long period. Several places noted their highest readings ever so late in the season (exceeding 90°F/32°C). A couple of heavy rain storms dropped readings back to seasonal levels in late-October. The first frosts occurred by November 7. November and December were marked by alternating cool and warm spells, though the warm spells lasted longer, and the result was both months averaged near to above normal (Figures 3 and 4). The season's first light snow came in the higher elevations to the west on December 6th. The year concluded with two weeks of quite mild weather.

Maps showing departures from average maximum daily temperatures (Figure 3) and average minimum temperatures (Figure 4) for each month in the calendar year 2007, as compared with the normal, based on the period 1971–2000 are illustrated. Departure values are reported in degrees Fahrenheit. Maps were created using estimates from the Parameter-elevation Regressions on Independent Slopes Model (PRISM). PRISM uses an interpolation scheme for temperature between actual observations and corrects these estimates for changes in topography across the region. More information can be found at: http://www.prism.oregonstate.edu/.

An upward temperature trend (Figure 5) and increase in the lowest annual temperature (Figure 6) can be observed for the parks over the past 30 years. There is no distinct trend in the growing season over a forty-year record for stations near the parks (Figure 7).

Table 4. Seasonal temperature and precipitation rankings over 114 years for VA Climate Division 2 for 2007. The values show the mildest and driest weather occurred in the autumn.

Climate Division Rankings – Virginia Climate Division 2	Jan–Feb–Mar WINTER	Apr–May–Jun SPRING	Jul–Aug–Sep SUMMER	Oct–Nov–Dec AUTUMN
Temperature-2007	33	42	18	8
Precipitation-2007	83	65	102	50

1 = Warmest or Wettest   114 = Coldest or Driest

Table 5. Summary of monthly average temperatures for 2007 from reporting sites that represent Petersburg NB and Richmond NBP.

Station Location	ID	Jan	Feb	Mar	Apr	May	Jun	Jul	Aug	Sep	Oct	Nov	Dec	Annual
Middle Peninsula, VA	KFYJ	5.31°C	1.73°C	11.18°C	13.46°C	19.38°C	23.88°C	25.13°C	25.78[d]°C	21.78°C	21.02°C	9.04[bc]°C	6.65°C	11.98°C
		41.56°F	35.12°F	52.13°F	56.23°F	66.89°F	74.98°F	77.23°F	78.41[d]°F	71.21°F	69.84°F	48.27[bc]°F	43.97°F	53.56°F
Hanover, VA	KOFP	6.03°C	1.42°C	10.91°C	13.36°C	19.26°C	23.66°C	24.82°C	26.10[d]°C	21.65°C	18.41°C	9.85°C	6.08°C	15.13°C
		42.85°F	34.55°F	51.63°F	56.04°F	66.66°F	74.58°F	76.68°F	78.99[d]°F	70.98°F	65.13°F	49.73°F	42.95°F	59.23°F
Richmond, VA	KRIC	6.67°C	2.01°C	11.11°C	14.15°C	19.58°C	24.32°C	25.40°C	26.44°C	22.34°C	19.12°C	9.85°C	6.60°C	15.63°C
		44.01°F	35.62°F	52.01°F	57.47°F	67.25°F	75.78°F	77.73°F	79.60°F	72.21°F	66.42°F	49.73°F	43.88°F	60.14°F
Wakefield, VA	KAKQ	6.51°C	2.13°C	10.49°C	13.65°C	18.67°C	23.34°C	24.65°C	25.78°C	21.44°C	18.30°C	8.91°C	7.59°C	15.12°C
		43.72°F	35.83°F	50.87°F	56.56°F	65.61°F	74.02°F	76.37°F	78.40°F	70.60°F	64.93°F	48.03°F	45.67°F	59.22°F
Mecklenburg, VA	KAVC	8.76°C	4.79°C	12.87°C	14.39°C	19.20°C	24.50°C	25.79°C	28.20[d]°C	23.56°C	20.25°C	11.55°C	9.49°C	16.94°C
		47.76°F	40.62°F	55.16°F	57.89°F	66.56°F	76.09°F	78.42°F	82.77[d]°F	74.42°F	68.46°F	52.78°F	49.08°F	62.50°F
Franklin, VA	KFKN	4.46°C	3.43°C	11.58°C	14.75°C	19.53°C	24.60°C	26.60°C	27.22[d]°C	22.74°C	19.61°C	9.96°C	8.29°C	16.32°C
		45.44°F	38.18°F	52.85°F	58.56°F	67.15°F	76.29°F	79.87°F	81.00[d]°F	72.94°F	67.30°F	49.92°F	46.93°F	61.37°F
Williamsburg, VA	KJGG	8.03°C	3.19°C	11.77°C	14.86°C	20.30°C	25.46°C	26.43°C	27.52[d]°C	23.68°C	22.26°C	12.55°C	8.48°C	17.04°C
		46.45°F	37.75°F	53.19°F	58.74°F	68.54°F	77.82°F	79.58°F	81.55[d]°F	74.62°F	72.08°F	54.60°F	47.26°F	62.68°F
Petersburg, VA	KPTB	7.53[d]°C	2.29[d]°C	11.73°C	13.82°C	19.57°C	24.03°C	25.44°C	26.74°C	21.81°C	17.83°C	9.17°C	6.59°C	15.55°C
		45.55[d]°F	36.12[d]°F	53.12°F	56.88°F	67.22°F	75.26°F	77.79°F	80.13°F	71.26°F	64.10°F	48.50°F	43.87°F	59.98°F
Camp Pickett, VA	CAPV2	5.32°C	0.88°C	10.53°C	12.76°C	18.66°C	23.23°C	24.54°C	26.42°C	21.97°C	17.74°C	8.73°C	6.03°C	14.74°C
		41.58°F	33.59°F	50.95°F	54.97°F	65.58°F	73.82°F	76.18°F	79.56°F	71.55°F	63.94°F	47.72°F	42.85°F	58.52°F
Emporia, VA	EPRV2	6.72°C	2.13°C	10.56°C	13.88°C	18.84°C	23.81°C	25.44°C	27.37°C	22.91°C	19.20°C	9.90°C	7.47°C	15.69°C
		44.10°F	35.84°F	51.02°F	56.98°F	65.90°F	74.87°F	77.79°F	81.27°F	73.23°F	66.56°F	49.82°F	45.45°F	60.24°F

[a] 1 day is missing, [b] 2 days missing, [c] 3 days missing, [d] 4 days missing
Monthly statistics not reported if more than 4 days are missing.

8

Table 6. Summary of departure from normal temperature based on 30-year normal (1971–2000) for 2007 from reporting sites that represent Petersburg NB and Richmond NBP.

Station Location	ID	Jan	Feb	Mar	Apr	May	Jun	Jul	Aug	Sep	Oct	Nov	Dec
Hanover, VA	KOFP	2.24°C	-2.97°C	2.21°C	-0.66°C	0.87°C	0.82°C	-0.09°C	1.54°C	1.1°C	3.91°C	0.27°C	1.19°C
		4.04°F	-5.34°F	3.98°F	-1.19°F	1.56°F	1.48°F	-0.16°F	2.76°F	1.98°F	7.03°F	0.50°F	2.14°F
Petersburg, VA	KPTB	3.12°C	-2.79°C	2.15°C	-1.30°C	-0.06°C	0.05°C	-0.48°C	1.34°C	0.42°C	2.55°C	-0.98°C	1.36°C
		5.61°F	-5.02°F	3.86°F	-2.35°F	-0.10°F	0.09°F	-0.86°F	2.42°F	0.76°F	4.58°F	-1.77°F	2.45°F
Richmond, VA	KRIC	4.23°C	-2.16°C	2.39°C	0.21°C	1.03°C	1.27°C	-0.07°C	1.84°C	1.34°C	4.52°C	0.41°C	1.94°C
		7.62°F	-3.88°F	4.30°F	0.37°F	1.86°F	2.28°F	-0.14°F	3.31°F	2.41°F	8.13°F	0.73°F	3.49°F
Williamsburg, VA	KJGG	4.43°C	-1.92°C	2.44°C	0.52°C	1.30°C	2.23°C	0.82°C	2.80°C	2.12°C	6.82°C	2.06°C	2.65°C
		7.97°F	-3.46°F	4.38°F	0.94°F	2.35°F	4.02°F	1.48°F	5.03°F	3.82°F	12.27°F	3.70°F	4.77°F
Camp Pickett, VA	CAPV2	3.32°C	-2.61°C	2.53°C	-0.23°C	0.82°C	0.90°C	-0.40°C	2.32°C	1.47°C	3.91°C	0.07°C	2.09°C
		5.97°F	-4.70°F	4.56°F	-0.43°F	1.48°F	1.62°F	-0.72°F	4.17°F	2.65°F	7.04°F	0.12°F	3.75°F
Emporia, VA	EPRV2	3.55°C	-2.53°C	1.57°C	-0.12°C	0.16°C	0.82°C	-0.06°C	2.82°C	1.79°C	4.42°C	0.23°C	2.36°C
		6.39°F	-4.55°F	2.83°F	-0.22°F	0.29°F	1.47°F	-0.11°F	5.08°F	3.23°F	7.95°F	0.42°F	4.26°F

Table 7. Status of 2007 temperature indicators compared to the 30-year normal (1971–2000) at Richmond, VA, weather observing station. The winter months brought seasonal chill with below average number of cold days. However, the summer of 2007 was above normal with the number of hot days (about 15% more hot days).

Temperature Indicators	Richmond, VA (KRIC) 2007	Richmond, VA (KRIC) 1971–2000
Cold Days (days with Tmax ≤ 32°F/0°C)	2	7.2
Sub-Freezing Nights (days with Tmin ≤ 32°F/0°C)	64	80.9
Cold Winter Nights (days with Tmin ≤ 0°F/17°C)	0	0.3
Hot Days (days with Tmax ≥ 90°F/32°C)	49	40.7
Growing Season Length (days between last 32°F/0°C in Spring and first 32°F/0°C in Fall)	212	200–210

Petersburg NB and Richmond NBP
Departure from Average Monthly Maximum Temperature
2007 vs. 1971–2000

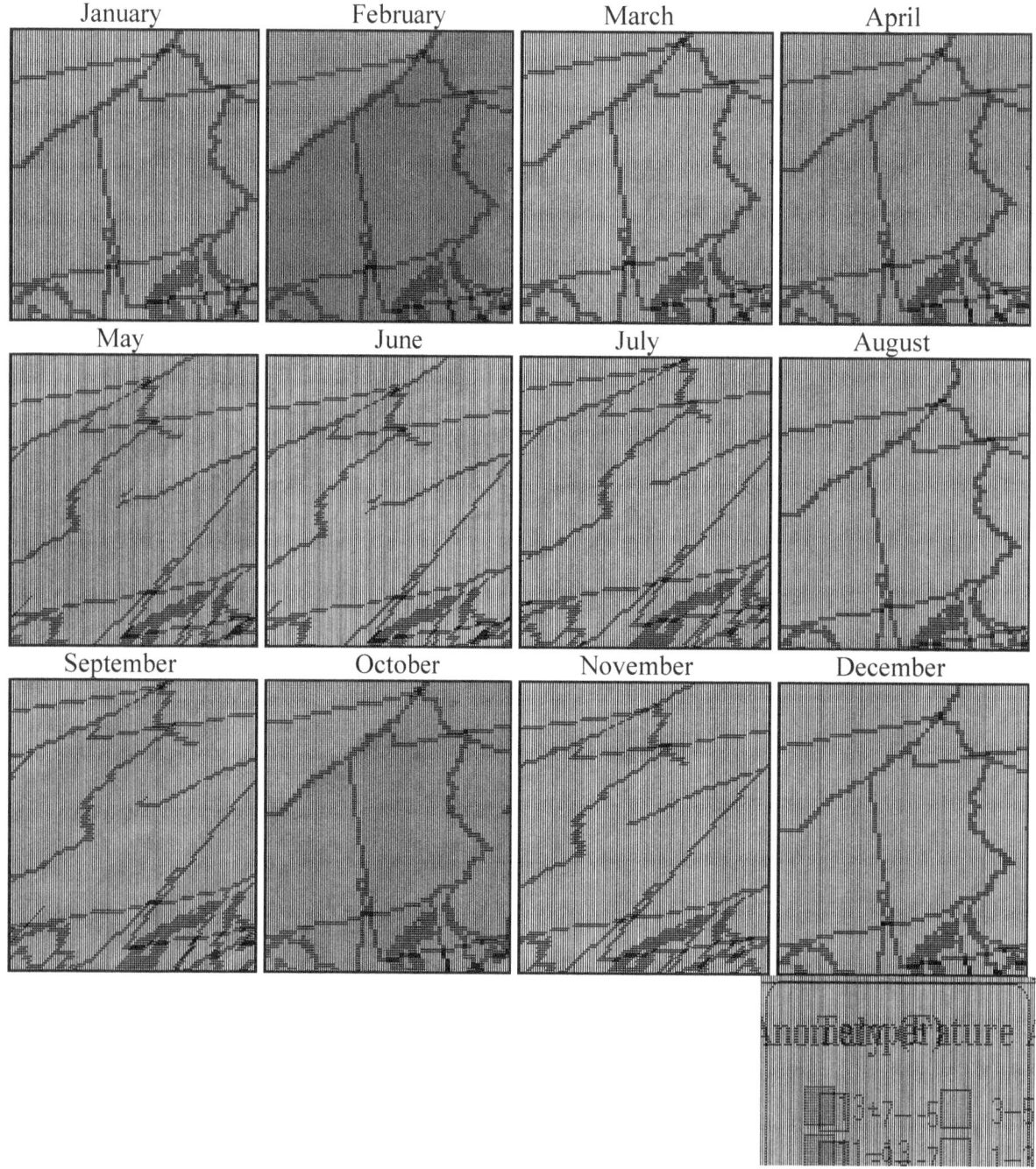

Figure 3. Maps showing departures from average maximum daily temperatures for each month in the calendar year 2007 as compared with the normal based on the period 1971–2000.

Petersburg NB and Richmond NBP
Departure from Average Monthly Minimum Temperature
2007 vs. 1971–2000

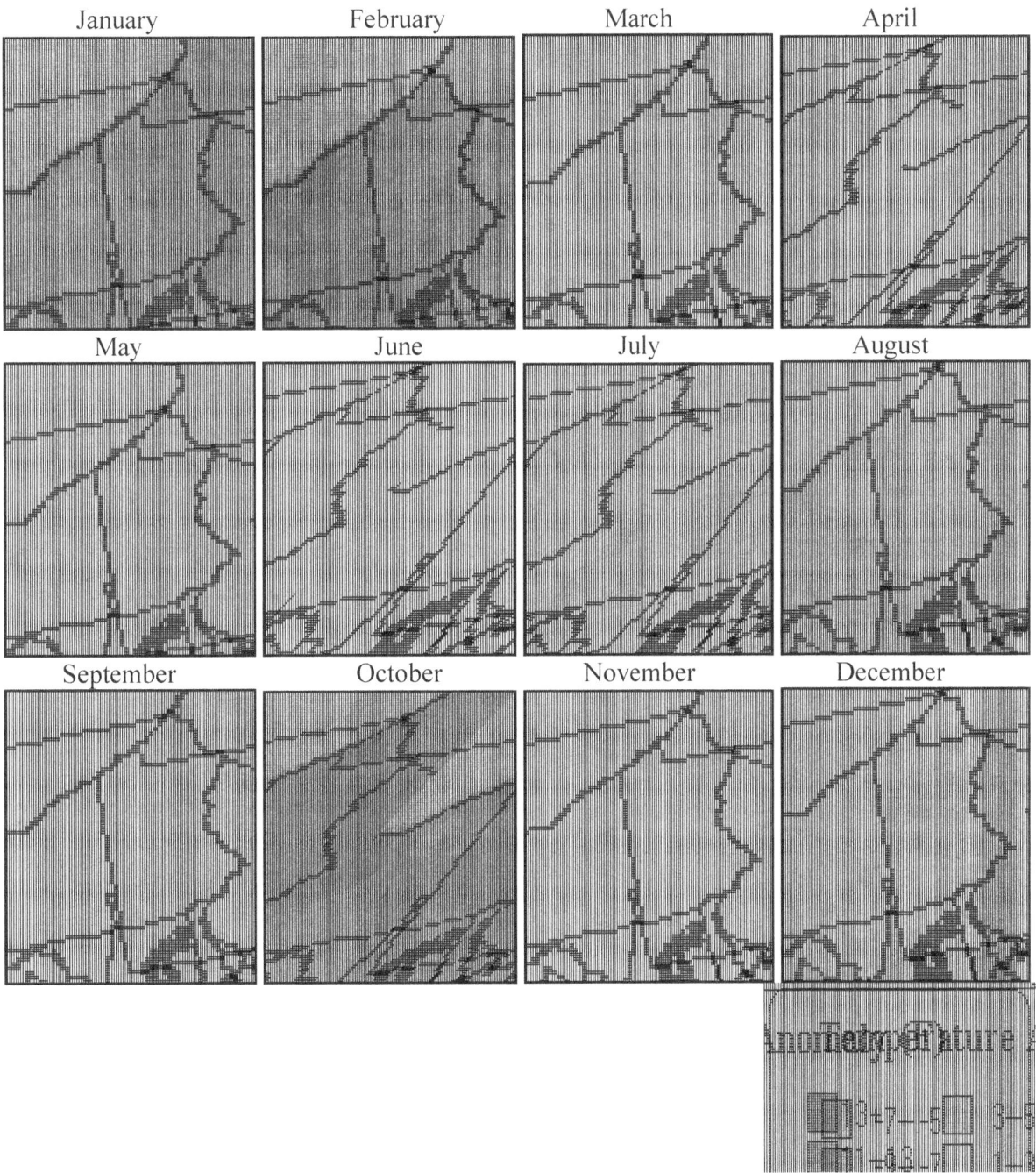

Figure 4. Maps showing departures from average minimum temperatures for each month in the calendar year 2007 as compared with the normal based on the period 1971–2000.

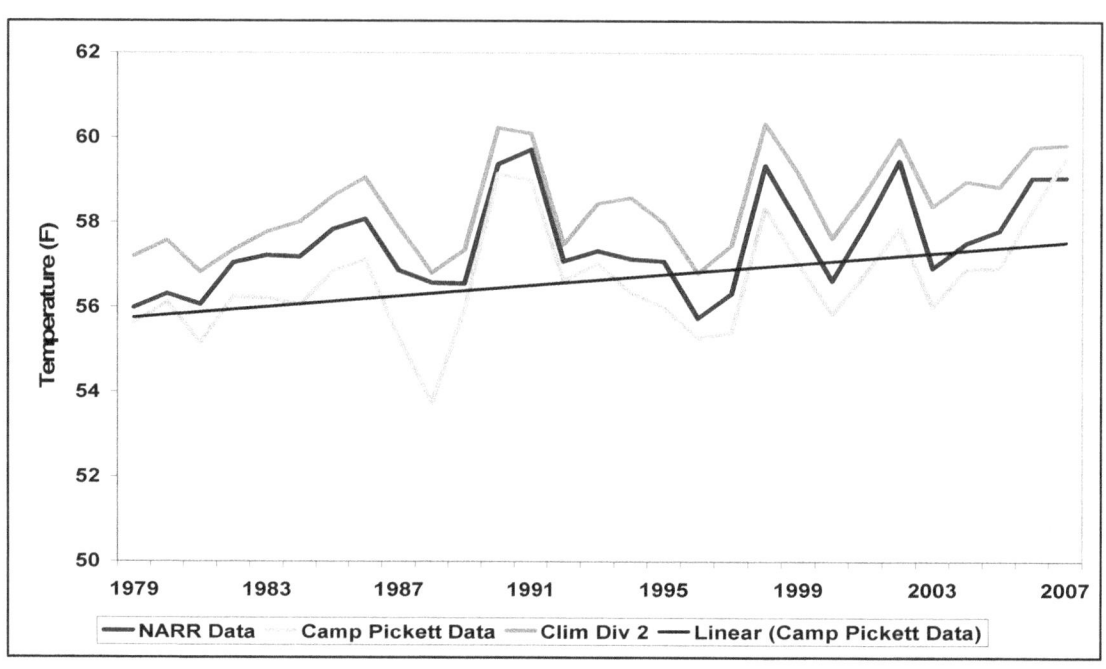

Figure 5. Annual temperature trends for Petersburg NB and Richmond NBP from 1979–2007. The red line shows VA Climate Division 2 data which are composed of more than 10 climate stations in the Virginia counties adjacent to the parks. The dark blue line is the temperature trend for a 32 km square box around PETE/RICH as derived from the North American Regional Reanalysis data set (NARR). This gridded database was the initial conditions for the numerical weather prediction models. The light blue shows the trend from a single Cooperative (COOP) weather station at Camp Pickett, VA. The agreement between all three data sources indicates the reliability of the NARR data as a good proxy for actual in-park observations. The temperature trend is upward at a rate of about 0.6°F (0.35°C) per decade.

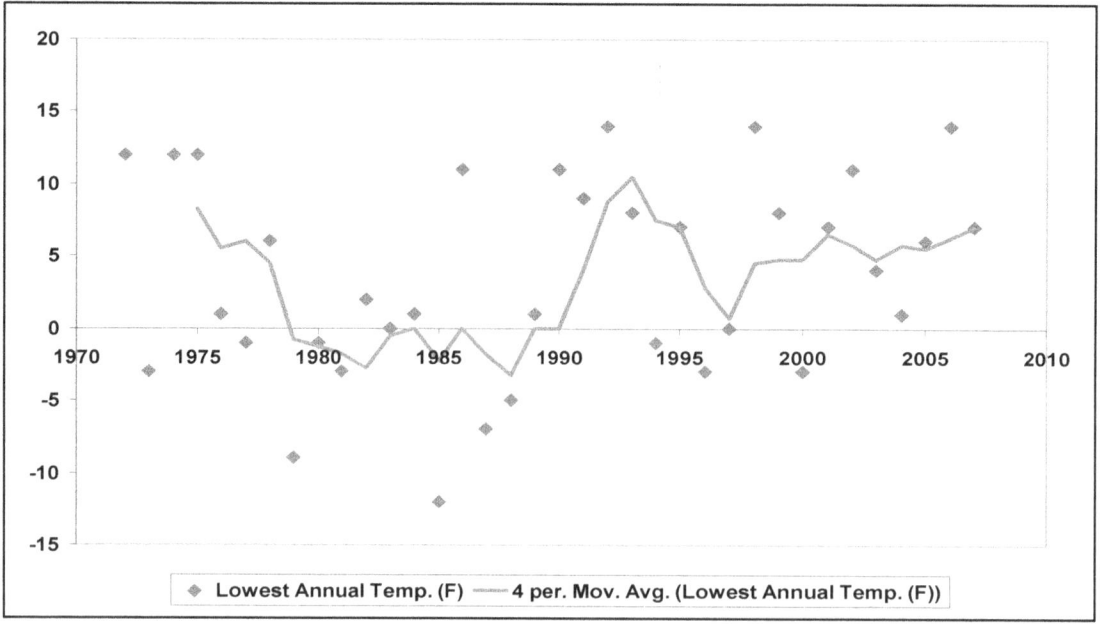

Figure 6. Representation of the lowest annual temperature trend for Petersburg NB and Richmond NBP from 1972–2007. The COOP site, Camp Pickett, VA, was used to determine this trend due to its long period of record and percent time of reporting. The last sub-zero reading occurred in 2000.

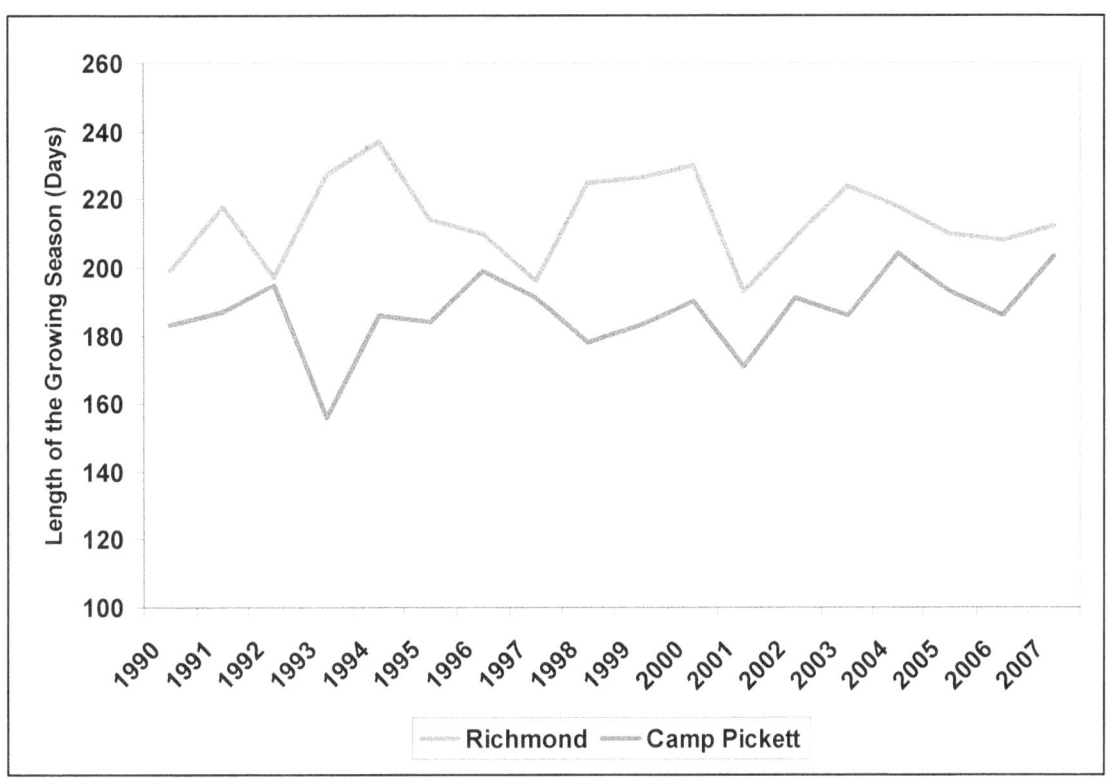

Figure 7. The growing season trend for Petersburg NB and Richmond NBP from 1990–2007. The number of days between the last freeze in the spring and the first freeze in the autumn does not show a distinct trend during the last decade as noted by two climate stations in proximity to the two parks.

Precipitation Summary

Both January and February were drier than average across the region (Figure 8). March also brought below average rainfall, but April featured a widespread rainstorm at mid-month caused by a powerful nor'easter (Table 8). Oddly, there was a significant precipitation event in the middle of the three months (Feb–Apr) of 2007. Most of these dropped more than an inch (25.4 mm) on the region.

The warm season of 2007 brought progressively drier conditions (Figure 8) due to greater evaporation rates. After a damp April, May saw significant rainfall on only a handful of days (Tables 9 and 10). More routine showers and thunderstorms returned in June, but the scattered nature of this rain left some sections with a deficit (Figure 8). July was quite dry as thunderstorms were widely separated. A bout of heavy thunderstorms in mid-August brought several reports of severe weather (Appendix) and also raised rainfall above the long-term mean for that month. Then from late August until mid October, rainfall was sparse with no contribution of moisture from the Tropics. Three long dry spells occurred during this period (Table 8). In fact, measurable rain occurred on less than 10 days from August 24–October 23. Rain returned in earnest starting on October 24 and the following three days produced more than 3.0 in (>75 mm) across the region. November saw a return to exceptionally dry weather (in fact, it was the driest on record in some locations of southern Virginia), but December had near normal rainfall.

Maps showing percent of average precipitation for each month in the calendar year 2007, as compared with the normal based on the period 1971–2000, are shown in Figure 8. Departure values are reported in percent of normal. Maps were created using estimates from the Parameter-elevation Regressions on Independent Slopes Model (PRISM). PRISM uses an interpolation scheme for precipitation between actual observations and corrects these estimates for changes in topography across the region. More information can be found at: http://www.prism.oregonstate.edu/.

Figure 9 provides the annual precipitation trends and Table 11 summarizes precipitation indicators for Petersburg NB and Richmond NBP.

Table 8. A comparison of wettest single calendar days during 2007 with the longest periods with a trace or less of rainfall during the same year in both parks.

Wettest Days in 2007	Dry Spells in 2007
Jan-01: 1.60 in (41 mm)	Oct. 6–23
Feb-14: 1.15 in (29 mm)	Sept. 16–Oct. 4
Mar-16: 1.61 in (41 mm)	Aug. 27–Sep. 10
Apr-15: 2.23 in (57 mm)	Feb. 15–24
Jun-30: 1.67 in (43 mm)	Mar. 17–28
Aug-16: 3.10 in (79 mm)	Mar. 3–14
Oct 24&26: 1.44 in (37 mm)	Feb. 2–11

Petersburg NB and Richmond NBP
Percent of Average Monthly Precipitation
2007 vs. 1971–2000

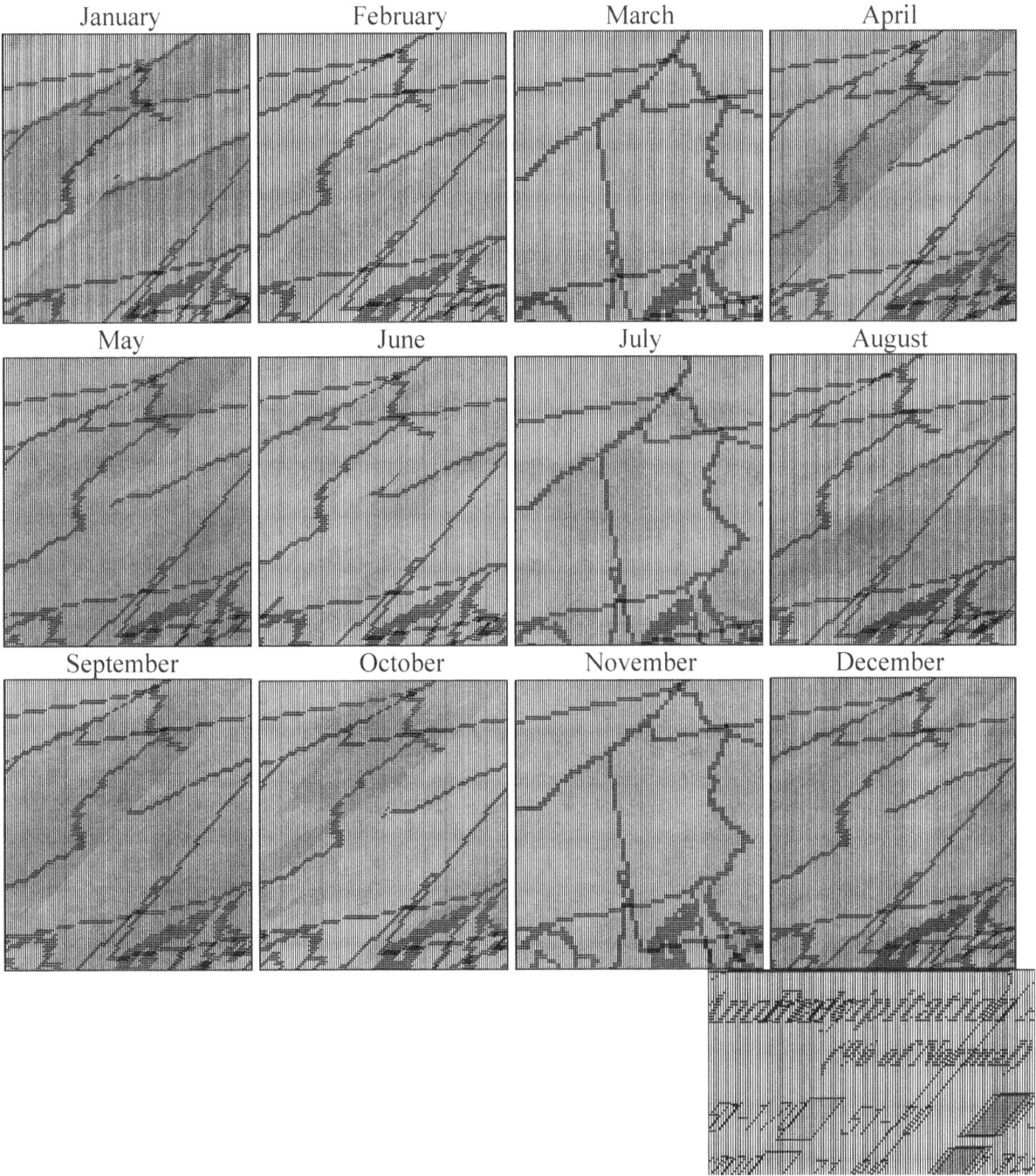

Figure 8. Maps showing percent of average precipitation for each month in the calendar year 2007 as compared with the normal based on the period 1971–2000.

Table 9. Summary of precipitation in 2007 for reporting sites that represent Petersburg NB and Richmond NBP.

Station Location	ID	Jan	Feb	Mar	Apr	May	Jun	Jul	Aug	Sep	Oct	Nov	Dec	Annual
Hanover, VA	KOFP	76.71 mm	68.07[b] mm	71.88 mm	80.01 mm	73.41 mm	91.19 mm	28.45 mm	50.29 mm	20.83 mm	89.92 mm	6.60[d] mm	73.91 mm	832.87 mm
		3.02 in	2.68[b] in	2.83 in	3.15 in	2.89 in	3.59 in	1.12 in	1.98 in	0.82 in	3.54 in	0.26[d] in	2.91 in	32.79 in
Richmond, VA	KRIC	87.12 mm	52.32 mm	63.50 mm	96.01 mm	94.23 mm	131.83 mm	42.93 mm	172.97 mm	28.19 mm	83.06 mm	15.75 mm	71.63 mm	939.55 mm
		3.43 in	2.06 in	2.50 in	3.78 in	3.71 in	5.19 in	1.69 in	6.81 in	1.11 in	3.27 in	0.62 in	2.82 in	36.99 in
Wakefield, VA	KAKQ	52.07 mm	46.48 mm	53.34 mm	150.88 mm	82.04 mm	116.33 mm	66.80 mm	180.85 mm	37.85 mm	101.35 mm	16.51 mm	102.11 mm	1006.60 mm
		2.05 in	1.83 in	2.10 in	5.94 in	3.23 in	4.58 in	2.63 in	7.12 in	1.49 in	3.99 in	0.65 in	4.02 in	39.63 in
Mecklenburg, VA	KAVC	48.01 mm	33.02 mm	61.21 mm	79.50 mm	48.01 mm	59.94 mm	30.73 mm	9.14[d] mm	18.03 mm	72.64 mm	2.29 mm	75.18 mm	537.72 mm
		1.89 in	1.30 in	2.41 in	3.13 in	1.89 in	2.36 in	1.21 in	0.36[d] in	0.71 in	2.86 in	0.09 in	2.96 in	21.17 in
Williamsburg, VA	KJGG	37.09 mm	37.85 mm	34.29 mm	78.99 mm	39.88 mm	38.10 mm	86.36 mm	51.31[d] mm	43.69 mm	72.90 mm	8.89 mm	64.77 mm	568.71 mm
		1.46 in	1.49 in	1.35 in	3.11 in	1.57 in	1.50 in	3.40 in	2.02[d] in	1.72 in	2.87 in	0.35 in	2.55 in	22.39 in
Petersburg, VA	KPTB	25.91 mm	37.85 mm	56.13 mm	76.45 mm	62.99 mm	58.17 mm	41.66 mm	78.99 mm	28.45 mm	88.39 mm	10.41 mm	75.18 mm	640.59 mm
		1.32[d] in	1.49[d] in	2.21 in	3.01c in	2.48 in	2.29 in	1.64 in	3.11 in	1.12 in	3.48 in	0.41 in	2.96 in	25.22 in
Camp Pickett, VA	CAPV2	71.88 mm	61.47 mm	79.50 mm	127.00 mm	96.01 mm	66.29 mm	103.63 mm	97.03 mm	25.40 mm	83.31 mm	25.91 mm	119.89 mm	1033.53 mm
		2.83 in	2.42 in	3.13 in	5.00 in	3.78 in	2.61 in	4.08 in	3.82 in	1.00 in	3.28 in	1.02 in	4.72 in	40.69 in
Emporia, VA	EPRV2	61.72 mm	46.48 mm	66.55 mm	77.22 mm	75.44 mm	76.20 mm	60.76 mm	74.68 mm	23.62 mm	84.58 mm	10.74 mm	124.74 mm	808.13 mm
		2.43 in	1.83 in	2.62 in	3.04 in	2.97 in	3.00 in	2.39 in	2.94 in	0.93 in	3.33 in	0.42 in	4.91 in	31.82 in

[a] 1 day is missing; [b] 2 days missing; [c] 3 days missing; [d] 4 days missing
Monthly statistics not reported if more than 4 days are missing

Table 10. Summary of 2007 percent of normal precipitation based on 30-year normal (1971–2000) for reporting sites that represent Petersburg NB and Richmond NBP.

Station Location	ID	Jan	Feb	Mar	Apr	May	Jun	Jul	Aug	Sep	Oct	Nov	Dec	Annual
Hanover, VA	KOFP	85	90	69	99	73	101	24	47	21	98	8	93	74
Petersburg, VA	KPTB	37	50	54	95	63	65	35	74	28	97	13	95	57
Richmond, VA	KRIC	97	69	61	119	94	147	36	162	28	91	20	90	84
Williamsburg, VA	KJGG	35	43	29	95	35	44	64	40	35	80	10	76	46
Camp Pickett, VA	CAPV2	66	75	73	137	92	68	93	91	24	83	31	148	87
Emporia, VA	EPRV2	61	58	63	91	77	91	53	68	22	96	14	161	72

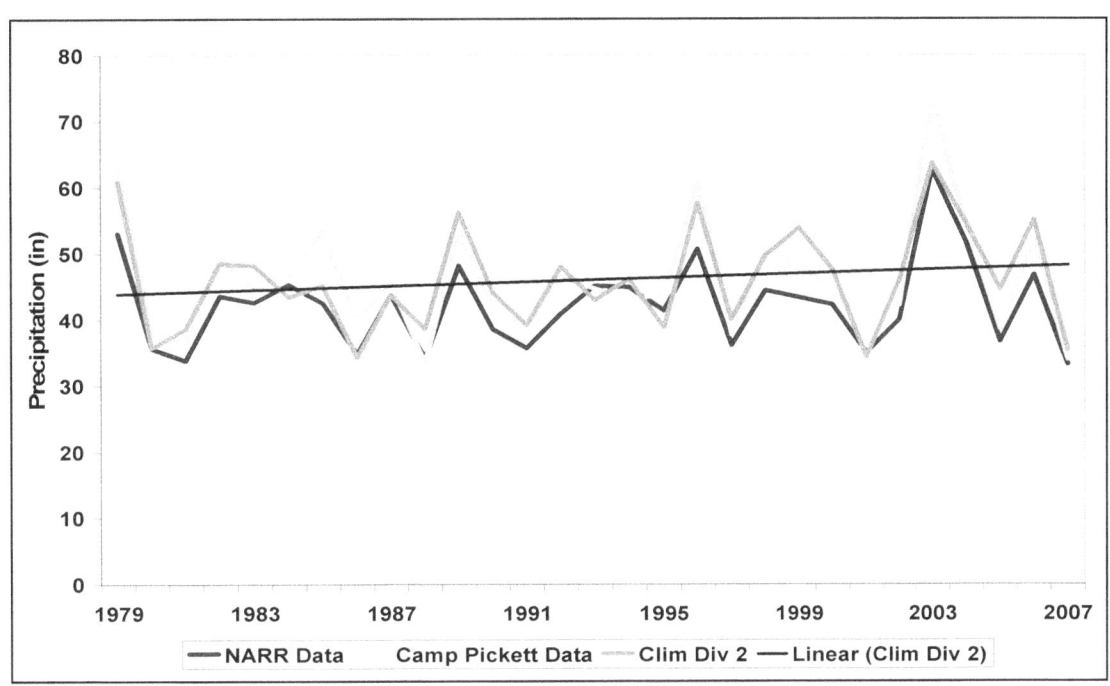

Figure 9. Annual precipitation trends for Petersburg NB and Richmond NBP from 1979–2007. The red line tracks the Climate Division data (Div #2 in Virginia) which represents an aggregate of more than 10 sites near the parks. The dark blue line marks the trend of a grid box around PETE/RICH from a North American Reanalysis data set. The light blue line shows the annual precipitation for a nearby single weather station, at Camp Pickett, VA. The 30-year trend shows an increase of nearly 7% (about ~3 in or 70 mm) since 1979.

Table 11. Status of 2007 precipitation indicators compared to the 30-year normal (1971–2000) at the Richmond station. The values in 2007 showed below normal annual rainfall and snowfall. Several long dry spells were also noted.

Precipitation Indicators	Richmond, VA (KRIC) 2007	Richmond, VA (KRIC) 30-year normal 1971–2000
Annual Precipitation	37.9	43.91
Annual Snowfall	1.3	12.4
Micro-drought (strings of 7+ days without rain)	9	-
Heavy Rain (days with ≥ 1.0 in / 25 mm rain)	10	11.5
Extreme Rain (days with ≥ 2.0 in / 51 mm rain)	3	-
Snow (days with ≥ 0.1 in / 0.3 cm snow)	2	-
Number of days with thunderstorms	27	-

Stream Flow

The USGS maintains river level and flow monitoring gauges along the James River. Of course, there is a response time between rainfall, snow-melt, and changes in the river conditions. There is also seasonality to the river flow with peak flows typically occurring in the spring and minimum flow being measured in the autumn. However, increases in precipitation amount and intensity during the past several decades have overridden some of this seasonality. Two gauges were selected to profile the river level and flow during the calendar year 2007 (Figures 10 and 11). Mid-month rainy spells show as regular spikes during the first half of 2007. The very dry November is noted by the very low flow rates

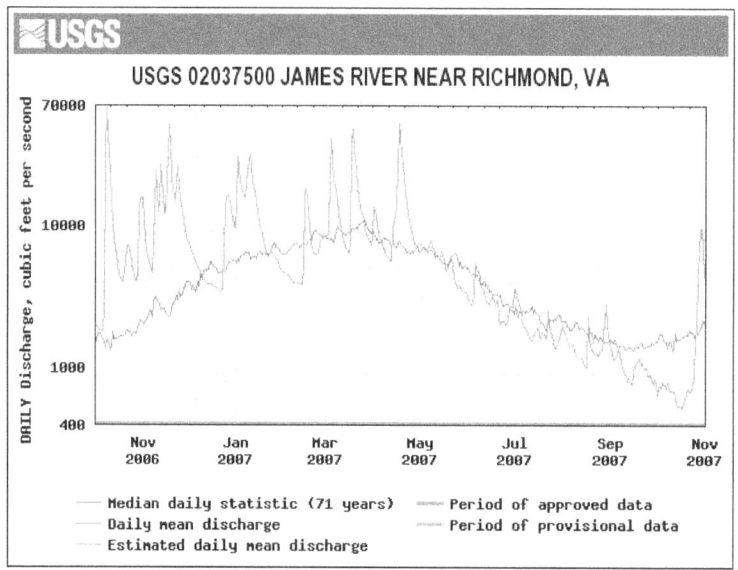

Figure 10. Discharge data for gage at James River near Richmond, VA.

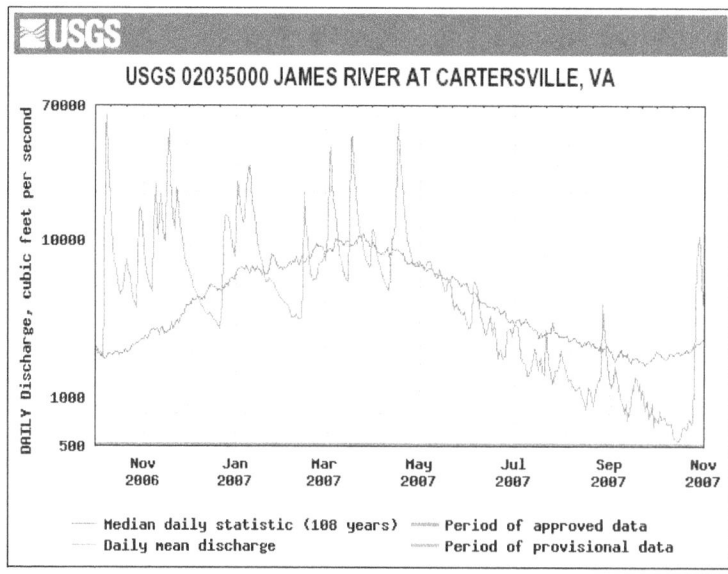

Figure 11. Discharge data for gage at James River near Cartersville, VA.

Drought Status

The U.S. Drought Monitor (USDM: http://www.drought.unl.edu/dm/monitor.html) tracks drought conditions across the nation on a weekly basis, and it incorporates data and expert input from a wide variety of state and federal agencies. The USDM is designed to represent a "broad brush," regional perspective on drought, and therefore provides an ideal tool for tracking generalized drought conditions across Southeastern Virginia parks and surrounding areas. According to the USDM, by the middle of April 2007, the Palmer Drought Severity Index (PDSI) began a steady drop from abnormally dry (~-1) to drought conditions (~-3) by late summer (Figure 12). These conditions persisted into the autumn. When compared with the past few years, 2007 was drier than either of those years and seems to have come under the influence of an extension of the longer-term Southeast U.S. drought. Since the PDSI responds to long-term effects, including evaporation, there is usually a lag between both long dry spells and episodes of heavy rain and changes in the index value. Comparative data is illustrated for Virginia (Figure 13) and the Southeast (Figure 14).

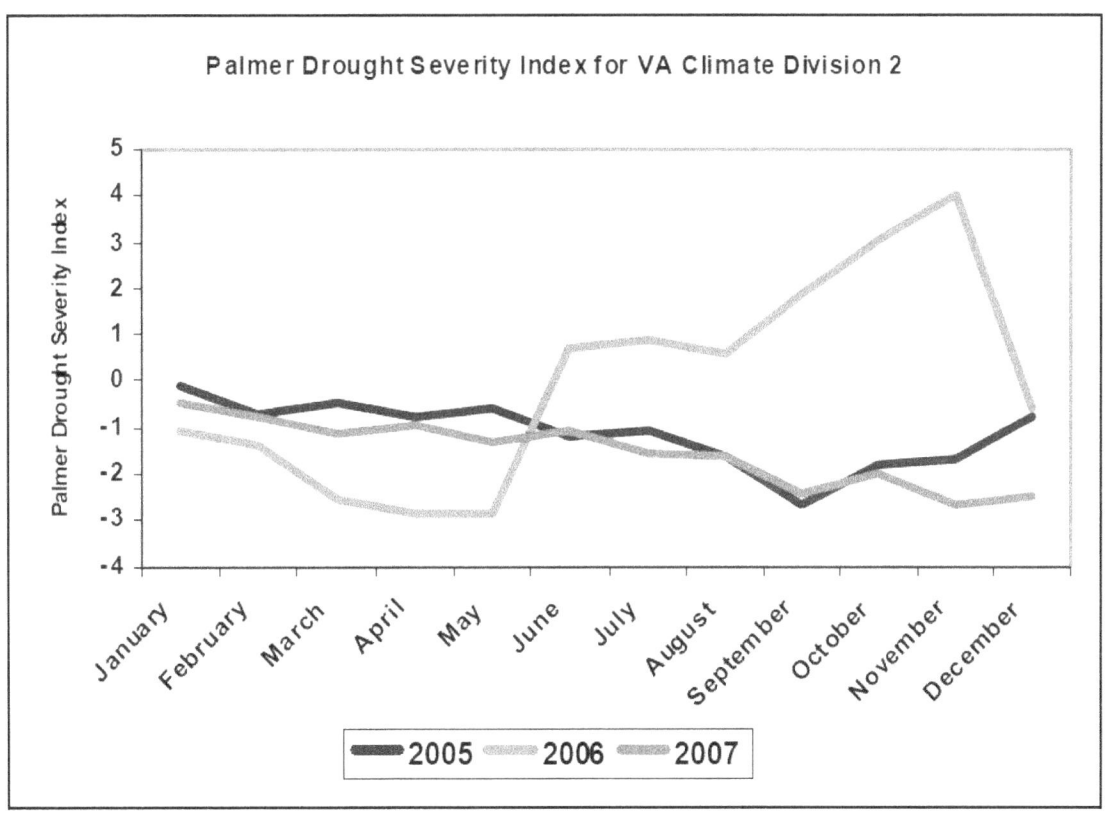

Figure 12. A comparison of the Palmer Drought Severity Index (PDSI) for the Virginia Climate Division 2 encompassing most of Petersburg NB and Richmond NBP from 2005–2007. The PDSI during 2007 was similar in dryness to 2005.

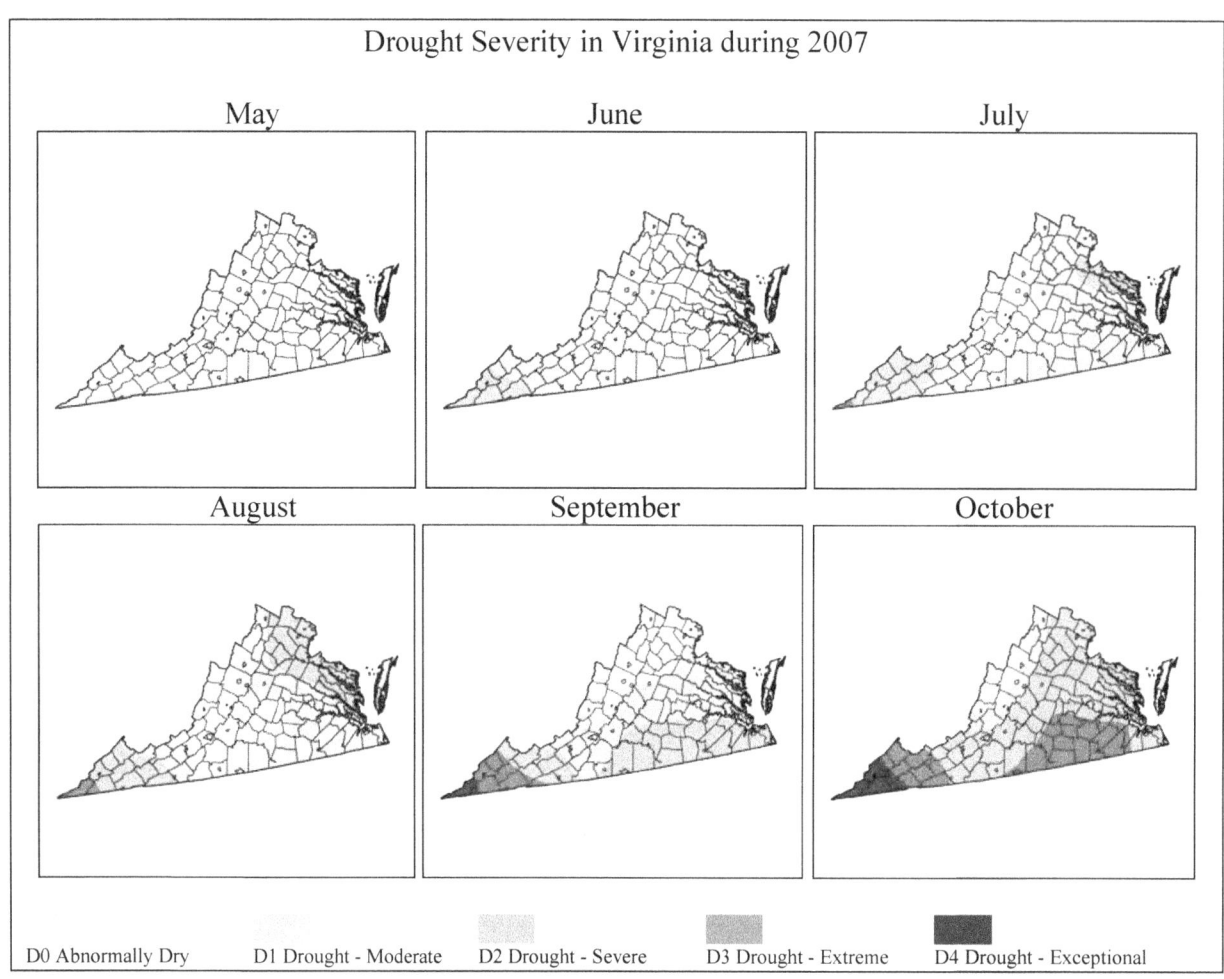

Figure 13. The mid-month values of the Palmer Drought Severity Index for Virginia in 2007 showing that dry conditions encroached on Petersburg NB and Richmond NBP.

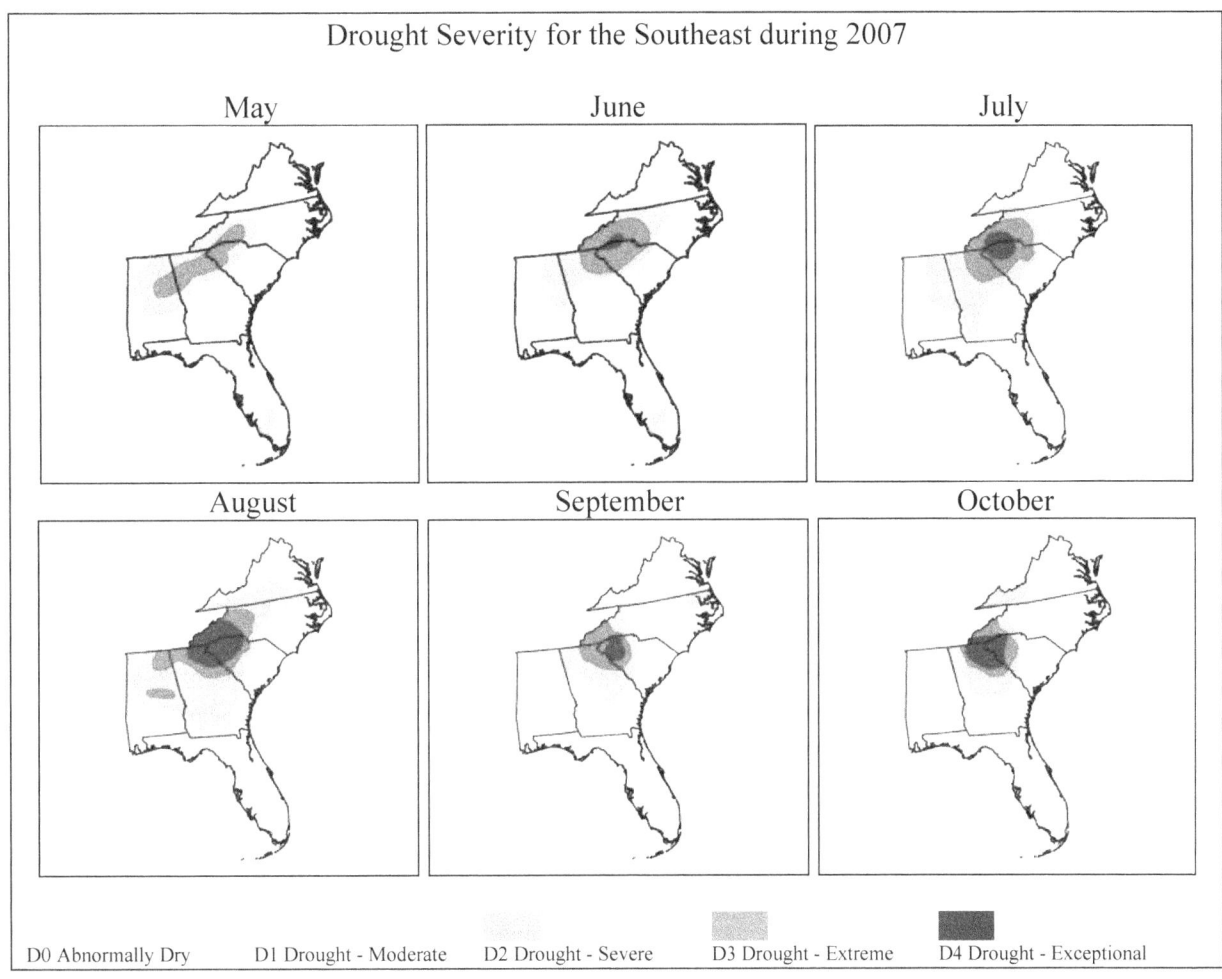

Figure 14. The mid-month values of the Palmer Drought Severity Index for the Southeast during the 2007 warm season.

Global and National Summary

Warmer-than-average temperatures occurred throughout 2007 in most land areas of the world, with the exception of cooler-than-average anomalies in the southern parts of South America (Figure 15). The largest warmer-than-average anomalies were present throughout high latitude regions of the Northern Hemisphere including much of North America, Europe, and Asia. Annual temperature anomalies in these regions ranged from 3.6–7.2°F (2–4°C) above the 1961–1990 average.

Notable temperature extremes in 2007 included a heat wave that affected a large portion of the United States throughout the month of August. The Central and Southeastern U.S. were particularly affected, with over 50 deaths attributed to soaring high temperatures. The anomalous warmth exacerbated drought conditions in the Southeastern region and also contributed for 29 all-time record high maximum temperatures and 35 all-time record high minimum temperatures.

In April, a devastating cold wave affected much of the central Plains, Midwest, and the Southeast region of the contiguous U.S. Temperatures dipped well below freezing in many areas prompting nearly 1,240 broken daily minimum temperature records and producing significant crop damages.

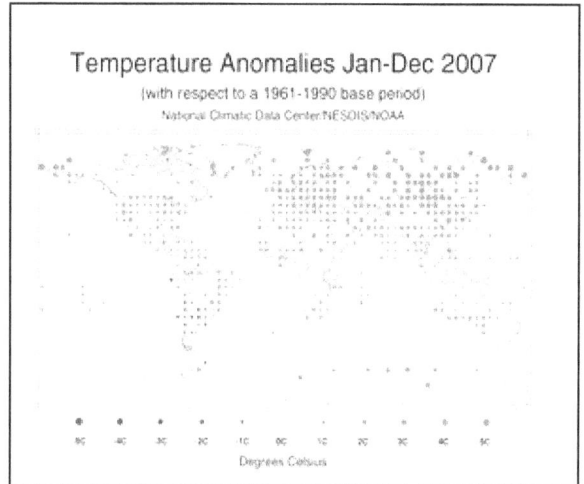

Annual Land Temperature Anomalies in degrees C

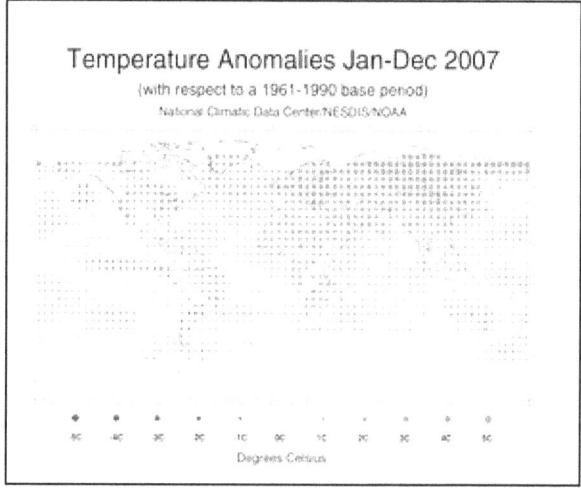

Annual Blended Land and Sea Temperature Anomalies in degrees C

Figure 15. Global temperature anomalies for 2007 with respect to a 1961–1990 base period. The map on left is created using data from the Global Historical Climatology Network (GHCN), a network of more than 7,000 land surface observing stations. The map on right is a product of a merged land surface and sea surface temperature anomaly analysis developed by Smith and Reynolds (2005). Temperature anomalies with respect to the 1961–1990 mean for land and ocean are analyzed separately and then merged to form the global analysis.

Snow cover for the boreal winter 2007 across North America was above average and was the 13th largest extent over the 41-year historical record (Figure 16). This was in part due to a series of snow and ice storms that struck the U.S. during the month of February. Average North America boreal winter snow cover extent is 17.0 million square kilometers for the 1967–2007 period of record.

Mean Northern Hemisphere snow cover extent during boreal spring (March–May) 2007 was below average (Figure 17). Much of this was due to anomalously warm conditions across Asia, Europe, and most of the contiguous U.S. Spring 2007 snow cover extent on the Northern Hemisphere was the third lowest extent on record. Mean Northern Hemisphere spring snow cover extent for the 1997–2007 period of record is 92.6 million square kilometers.

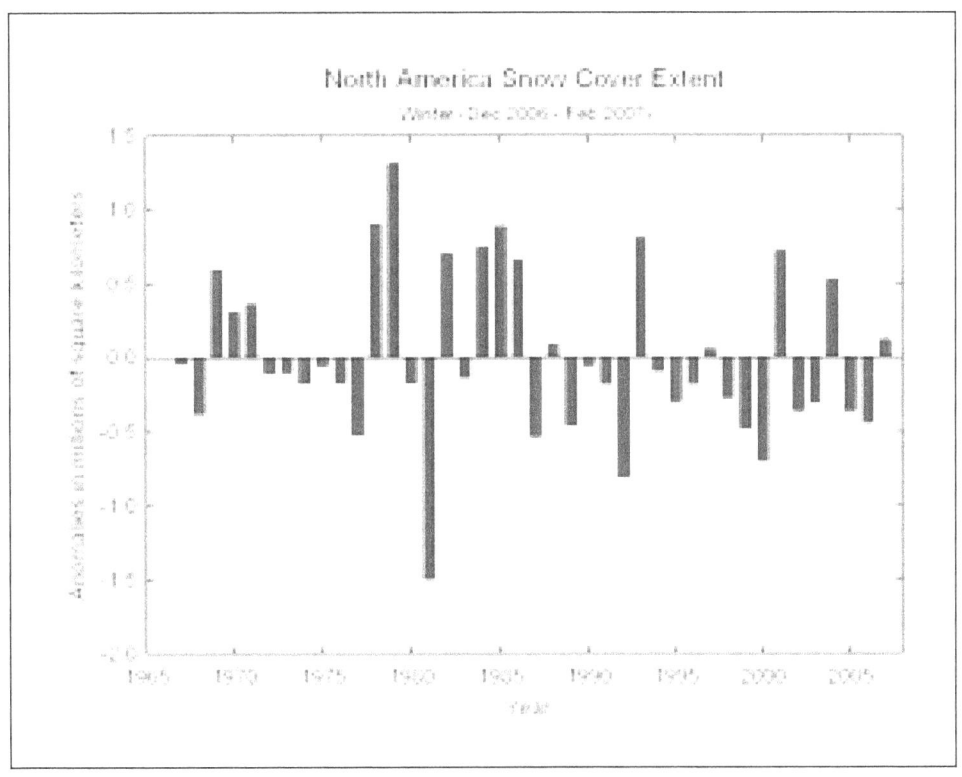

Figure 16. North American snow cover anomalies for 1967–2007 winters (Dec.–Feb.).

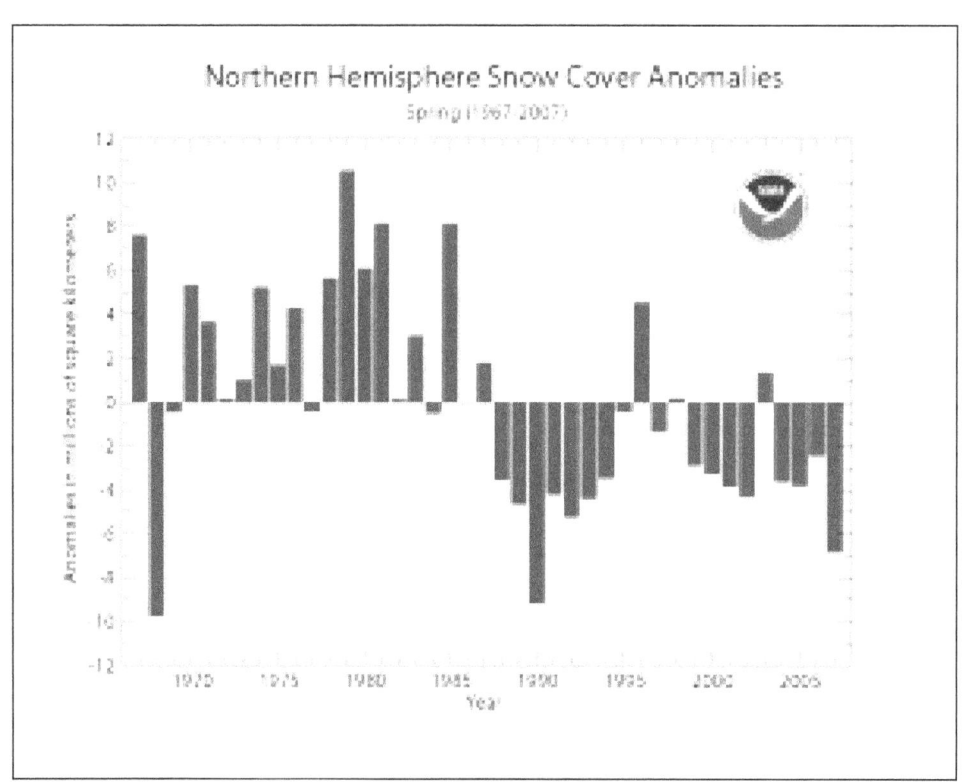

Figure 17. Northern Hemisphere snow cover anomalies for 1967–2007 spring (March–May).

Based on data through the end of the year, 2007 was the tenth warmest year on record for the U.S., with a nationally averaged temperature of 54.2°F (12.4°C). This value is 1.4°F (0.8°C) above the 20th century (1901–2000) mean.

Much warmer-than-average temperatures affected much of the mountain west and parts of the east during 2007. This was the tenth warmest January–December in the 113-year record. Both Kentucky and Tennessee had the fourth warmest years on record. Forty-three of the lower 48 states were either warmer or much warmer than average in 2007. Maine alone ranked below average during the 2007 year-to-date period. The anomalous warmth affecting the U.S. in 2007 is also reflected in temperatures in the lower troposphere. Data collected by NOAA's TIROS-N polar-orbiting satellites and adjusted for time-dependent biases by NASA and the Global Hydrology and Climate Center at the University of Alabama in Huntsville indicate that temperatures in the lower half of the atmosphere (lowest 8 km of the atmosphere) over the U.S. were warmer than the 20-year (1979–1998) average for the tenth consecutive year.

Precipitation in the United States during 2007 was variable throughout much of the country with periods of excessive rainfall, especially across the central third of the U.S., and persistent and developing drought in the southeastern quarter of the country and the far western states. Winter was relatively wet in the South and North Central regions and relatively dry in the West and Southeast (Figures 19 and 20). In the spring, it was the driest March–May on record in the Southeast.

The West was ranked sixth driest and the West North Central region had its third wettest spring on record. In summer, the remnants of Tropical Storm Erin brought excessive rain to Texas, Oklahoma, and Kansas, giving the South its wettest summer on record. Meanwhile, much of the Southeast continued to suffer in drought with its eleventh driest summer on record, following the driest spring.

Precipitation across the U.S. during the fall ranked 37th driest, although no regions ranked much above or much below normal. For the contiguous U.S. as a whole, seven months in 2007 were drier than average. The annual temperature trend for the nation based on the historical climate network (USHCN) shows that 2007 was down slightly from 2006, but still ranked as tied for the sixth warmest year in the past century.

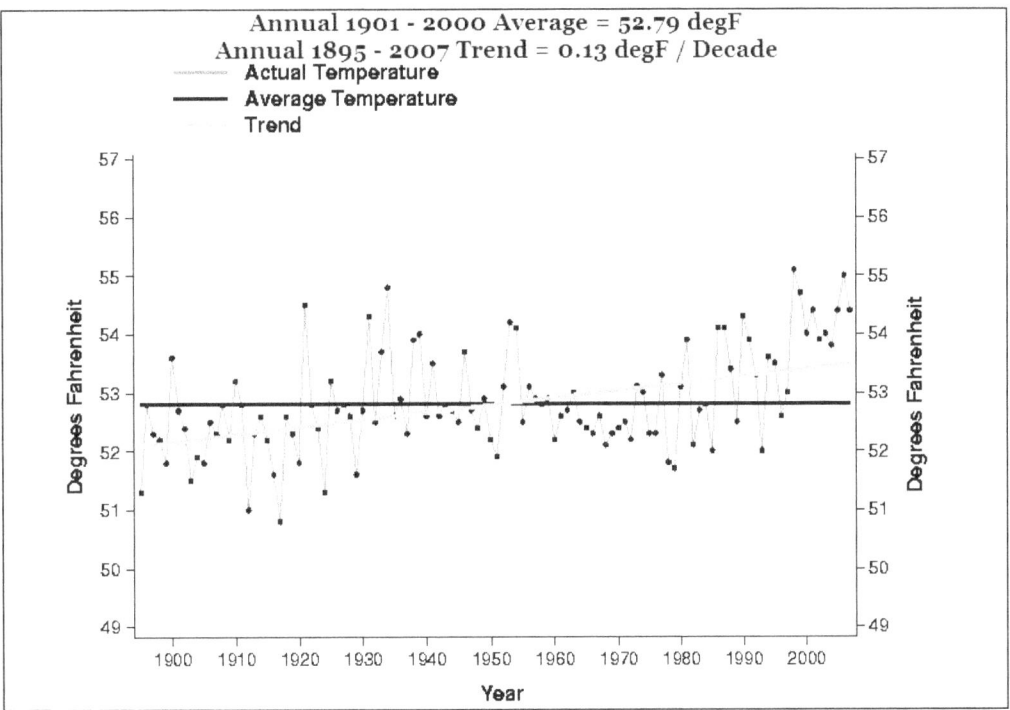

Figure 18. The long-term annual temperature trend for the United States based on the Historical Climate Network (HCN) which is a subset of the Cooperative Network of Weather Observers.

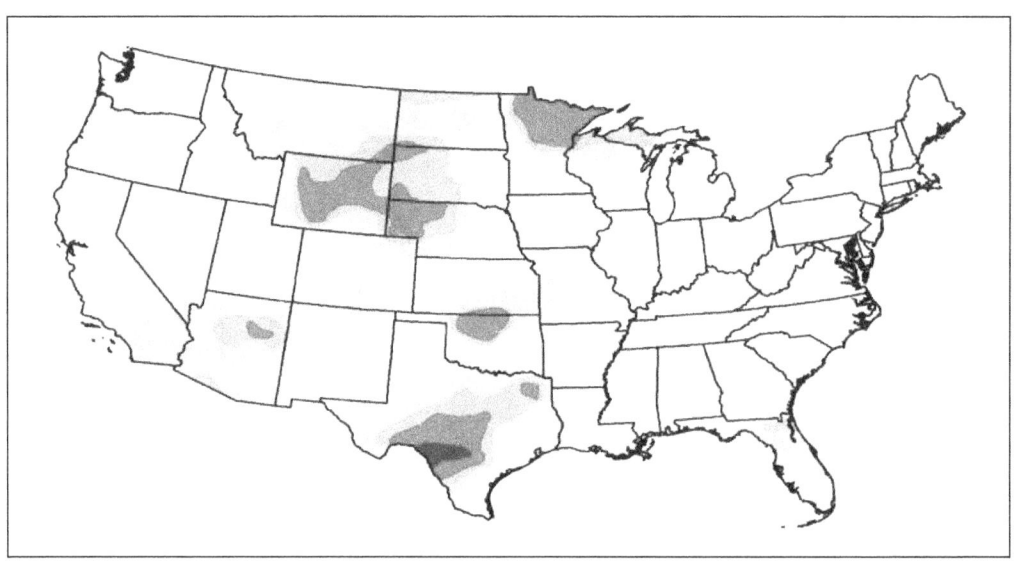

Figure 19. Palmer Drought Severity Index for January 2, 2007. The majority of the Plains were experiencing abnormally dry to moderate drought conditions.

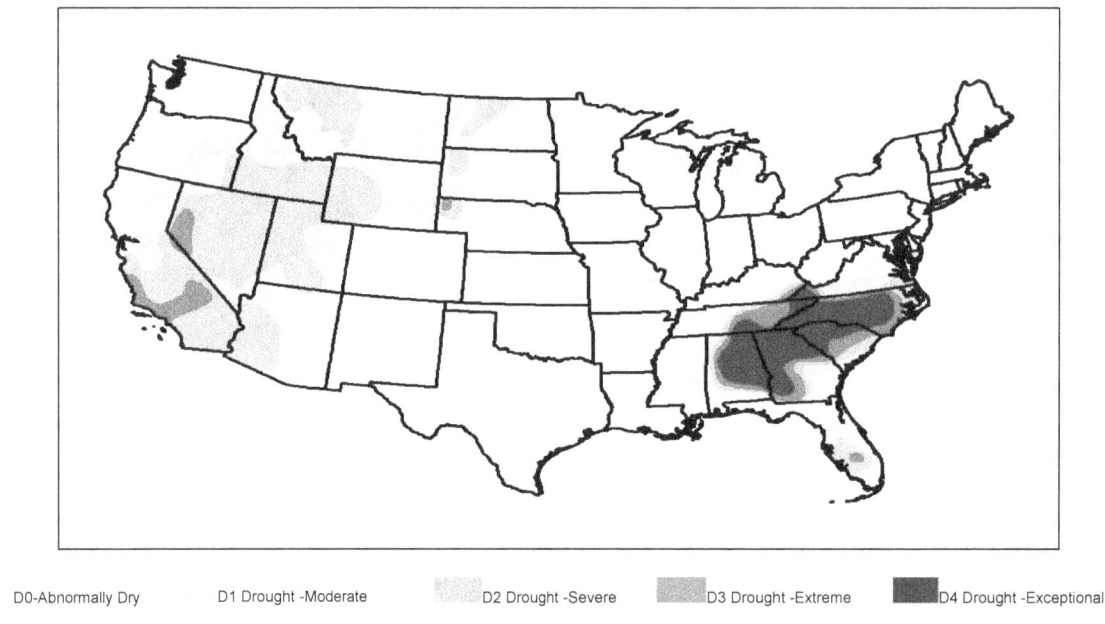

D0-Abnormally Dry   D1 Drought -Moderate   D2 Drought -Severe   D3 Drought -Extreme   D4 Drought -Exceptional

Figure 20. Palmer Drought Severity Index for December 25, 2007. The center of intensely dry weather had settled into the Southeast United States.

Selected References

Davey, C. A., K. T. Redmond, and D. B. Simeral. 2006. Weather and Climate Inventory, National Park Service, Mid-Atlantic Network. Natural Resource Technical Report NPS/MIDN/NRTR—2006/013. National Park Service, Fort Collins, Colorado.

Knight, P., T. Wisniewski, C. Bahrmann, and S. Miller. In preparation. Weather and Climate Monitoring Protocol for the Eastern Rivers and Mountains and Mid-Atlantic Networks. Natural Resource Technical Report NPS/MIDN/NRTR—2010/XXX. National Park Service, Fort Collins, CO.

National Oceanic and Atmospheric Administration (NOAA). 2007. National Climatic Data Center. Climate of 2007 – Annual Review, Global and U.S. Summary, http://lwf.ncdc.noaa.gov/oa/climate/research/2007/ann/us-summary.html.

Smith, T. M. and Reynolds, R. W. 2005 A Global Merged Land—Air—Sea Surface Temperature Reconstruction Based on Historical Observations (1880-1997). Journal of Climate, 18, 2021-2036.

27

Appendix

The following tables are a tally of all reports of severe weather during 2007 in the counties that encompass Petersburg National Battlefield and Richmond National Battlefield Park. These storm events were provided by the National Climatic Data Center (NCDC). NCDC receives this storm data from the National Weather Service, who acquires their information from a variety of sources. These sources include but are not limited to: county, state and federal emergency management officials, local law enforcement officials, skywarn spotters, NWS damage surveys, newspaper clipping services, the insurance industry and the general public. This Storm Data is an official publication of the National Oceanic and Atmospheric Administration (NOAA 2007) which documents the occurrence of storms and other significant weather phenomena having sufficient intensity to cause loss of life, injuries, significant property damage, and/or disruption to commerce. Each table contains the location, date, time, and description of the severe event, its magnitude, and number of deaths and injuries, and property/crop damage associated with the event. The property and crop damage should be considered as a broad estimate.

Petersburg City County

Location or County	Date	Time	Type	Mag	Dth	Inj	PrD	CrD
1 Petersburg	06/28/2007	19:10 PM	Thunderstorm Wind	50 kts.	0	0	2K	0K
2 Petersburg	07/19/2007	15:00 PM	Thunderstorm Wind	50 kts.	0	0	1K	0K
3 Petersburg	10/24/2007	12:00 PM	Heavy Rain	N/A	0	0	0K	0K
				TOTALS:	0	0	3K	0

Mag: Magnitude; Dth: Deaths; Inj: Injuries; PrD: Property Damage; CrD: Crop Damage.

Nottoway County

Location or County	Date	Time	Type	Mag	Dth	Inj	PrD	CrD
1 Burkeville	06/11/2007	15:50 PM	Thunderstorm Wind	50 kts.	0	0	1K	0K
2 Jennings Ordinary	08/21/2007	16:10 PM	Thunderstorm Wind	50 kts.	0	0	1K	0K
3 Crewe	10/24/2007	12:00 PM	Heavy Rain	N/A	0	0	0K	0K
				TOTALS:	0	0	2K	0

Mag: Magnitude; Dth: Deaths; Inj: Injuries; PrD: Property Damage; CrD: Crop Damage.

Meclenburg County

Location or County	Date	Time	Type	Mag	Dth	Inj	PrD	CrD
1 Clarksville	06/04/2007	21:00 PM	Thunderstorm Wind	50 kts.	0	0	2K	0K
2 South Hill	10/24/2007	12:00 PM	Heavy Rain	N/A	0	0	0K	0K
				TOTALS:	0	0	2K	0

Mag: Magnitude; Dth: Deaths; Inj: Injuries; PrD: Property Damage; CrD: Crop Damage.

James City County

Location or County	Date	Time	Type	Mag	Dth	Inj	PrD	CrD
1 VAZ049 - 064 - 072 - 076>078 - 084>085 - 090 - 099	04/07/2007	03:00 AM	Heavy Snow	N/A	0	0	0K	0K
2 VAZ049 - 064 - 072 - 076>078 - 084>085 - 090 - 099	04/07/2007	03:00 AM	Winter Weather	N/A	0	0	0K	0K
3 Five Forks	06/29/2007	19:02 PM	Hail	1.00 in.	0	0	0K	0K
4 Grove	06/29/2007	19:05 PM	Thunderstorm Wind	50 kts.	0	0	10K	0K
5 Grove	06/29/2007	19:15 PM	Hail	1.00 in.	0	0	0K	250K
6 Five Forks	06/29/2007	19:30 PM	Thunderstorm Wind	60 kts.	0	0	1.0M	0K
7 Toano	07/11/2007	17:45 PM	Thunderstorm Wind	50 kts.	0	0	1K	0K
8 Jamestown	07/19/2007	15:35 PM	Thunderstorm Wind	50 kts.	0	0	5K	0K
9 Toano	07/19/2007	15:40 PM	Thunderstorm Wind	50 kts.	0	0	1K	0K
10 Norge	08/05/2007	16:50 PM	Thunderstorm Wind	50 kts.	0	0	2K	0K
11 Jamestown	10/24/2007	12:00 PM	Heavy Rain	N/A	0	0	0K	0K
				TOTALS:	0	0	1.019M	250K

Mag: Magnitude; Dth: Deaths; Inj: Injuries; PrD: Property Damage; CrD: Crop Damage.

Greensville County

Location or County	Date	Time	Type	Mag	Dth	Inj	PrD	CrD
1 Purdy	10/24/2007	12:00 PM	Heavy Rain	N/A	0	0	0K	0K
				TOTALS:	0	0	0	0

Mag: Magnitude; Dth: Deaths; Inj: Injuries; PrD: Property Damage; CrD: Crop Damage.

Chesterfield County

Location or County	Date	Time	Type	Mag	Dth	Inj	PrD	CrD
1 Midlothian	06/08/2007	21:18 PM	Hail	1.00 in.	0	0	0K	0K
2 Chester	06/27/2007	17:09 PM	Hail	0.88 in.	0	0	0K	0K
3 Winterpock	07/17/2007	16:30 PM	Thunderstorm Wind	50 kts.	0	0	1K	0K
4 Matoaca	07/17/2007	16:40 PM	Thunderstorm Wind	50 kts.	0	0	1K	0K
5 Chester	07/19/2007	14:50 PM	Thunderstorm Wind	50 kts.	0	0	1K	0K
6 Midlothian	07/19/2007	19:42 PM	Thunderstorm Wind	50 kts.	0	0	1K	0K
7 Midlothian	08/16/2007	20:40 PM	Thunderstorm Wind	50 kts.	0	0	1K	0K
8 Chesterfield	08/16/2007	20:50 PM	Hail	0.75 in.	0	0	0K	0K
9 Chesterfield Co Arpt	08/16/2007	20:50 PM	Thunderstorm Wind	50 kts.	0	0	1K	0K
10 Midlothian	08/16/2007	20:50 PM	Thunderstorm Wind	50 kts.	0	0	1K	0K
11 Chesterfield	08/16/2007	20:55 PM	Thunderstorm Wind	50 kts.	0	0	1K	0K
12 Chester	08/16/2007	22:17 PM	Hail	0.88 in.	0	0	0K	0K
13 Beach	08/17/2007	12:45 AM	Flash Flood	N/A	0	0	0K	0K
14 Bellbluff	08/17/2007	02:10 AM	Flash Flood	N/A	0	0	0K	0K
15 Chesterfield	08/19/2007	20:15 PM	Thunderstorm Wind	50 kts.	0	0	1K	0K
16 Matoaca	08/19/2007	20:15 PM	Thunderstorm Wind	50 kts.	0	0	2K	0K
17 Matoaca	08/21/2007	16:38 PM	Thunderstorm Wind	50 kts.	0	0	1K	0K
18 Midlothian	08/21/2007	16:50 PM	Thunderstorm Wind	50 kts.	0	0	1K	0K
19 Midlothian	10/24/2007	12:00 PM	Heavy Rain	N/A	0	0	0K	0K
				TOTALS:	0	0	13K	0

Mag: Magnitude; Dth: Deaths; Inj: Injuries; PrD: Property Damage; CrD: Crop Damage.

New Kent County

Location or County	Date	Time	Type	Mag	Dth	Inj	PrD	CrD
1 Quinton	05/28/2007	18:45 PM	Thunderstorm Wind	50 kts.	0	0	2K	0K
2 New Kent	07/19/2007	15:00 PM	Thunderstorm Wind	50 kts.	0	0	1K	0K
3 Lanexa	07/19/2007	15:15 PM	Thunderstorm Wind	50 kts.	0	0	1K	0K
4 Quinton Arpt	08/05/2007	14:08 PM	Thunderstorm Wind	50 kts.	0	0	1K	0K
5 Quinton	08/10/2007	01:15 AM	Thunderstorm Wind	50 kts.	0	0	1K	0K
6 New Kent	10/24/2007	12:00 PM	Heavy Rain	N/A	0	0	0K	0K
				TOTALS:	0	0	6K	0

Mag: Magnitude; Dth: Deaths; Inj: Injuries; PrD: Property Damage; CrD: Crop Damage.

Hanover County

Location or County	Date	Time	Type	Mag	Dth	Inj	PrD	CrD
1 VAZ048 - 063>064 - 072>078 - 085>086 - 099	01/21/2007	11:00 AM	Winter Weather	N/A	0	0	0K	0K
2 VAZ048 - 060 - 062>064 - 072 - 074	02/13/2007	17:00 PM	Winter Storm	N/A	0	0	10K	0K
3 VAZ048 - 060 - 062>064 - 072 - 074	02/13/2007	17:00 PM	Winter Weather	N/A	0	0	0K	0K
4 Mechanicsville	05/28/2007	18:26 PM	Hail	0.75 in.	0	0	0K	0K
5 Mechanicsville	05/28/2007	18:32 PM	Thunderstorm Wind	50 kts.	0	0	2K	0K
6 Mechanicsville	06/11/2007	13:55 PM	Hail	0.88 in.	0	0	0K	0K
7 Mechanicsville	06/11/2007	13:58 PM	Hail	1.00 in.	0	0	0K	0K
8 Montpelier	07/16/2007	15:15 PM	Hail	1.00 in.	0	0	0K	0K
9 Peaks	08/10/2007	01:00 AM	Thunderstorm Wind	50 kts.	0	0	1K	0K
10 Ashland	08/16/2007	18:40 PM	Thunderstorm Wind	50 kts.	0	0	1K	0K
11 Mechanicsville	08/19/2007	18:55 PM	Thunderstorm Wind	50 kts.	0	0	2K	0K
12 Mechanicsville	08/19/2007	22:40 PM	Thunderstorm Wind	50 kts.	0	0	1K	0K
13 Ashland	08/21/2007	17:05 PM	Thunderstorm Wind	50 kts.	0	0	1K	0K
14 Montpelier	08/21/2007	17:10 PM	Thunderstorm Wind	50 kts.	0	0	1K	0K
15 Mechanicsville	08/21/2007	17:15 PM	Thunderstorm Wind	50 kts.	0	0	1K	0K
16 Studley	08/21/2007	17:18 PM	Thunderstorm Wind	50 kts.	0	0	1K	0K
17 Studley	08/21/2007	17:25 PM	Thunderstorm Wind	50 kts.	0	0	1K	0K
18 Farrington	10/24/2007	12:00 PM	Heavy Rain	N/A	0	0	0K	0K
				TOTALS:	0	0	22K	0

Mag: Magnitude; Dth: Deaths; Inj: Injuries; PrD: Property Damage; CrD: Crop Damage.

King and Queen County

Location or County	Date	Time	Type	Mag	Dth	Inj	PrD	CrD
1 VAZ048 - 063>064 - 072>078 - 085>086 - 099	01/21/2007	11:00 AM	Winter Weather	N/A	0	0	0K	0K
2 Newtown	05/02/2007	15:30 PM	Lightning	N/A	0	0	2K	0K
3 Newtown	05/02/2007	15:30 PM	Thunderstorm Wind	50 kts.	0	0	2K	0K
4 Little Plymouth	10/24/2007	12:00 PM	Heavy Rain	N/A	0	0	0K	0K
				TOTALS:	0	0	4K	0

Mag: Magnitude; Dth: Deaths; Inj: Injuries; PrD: Property Damage; CrD: Crop Damage.

34

Henrico County

Location or County	Date	Time	Type	Mag	Dth	Inj	PrD	CrD
1 Yellow Tavern	06/08/2007	21:12 PM	Hail	0.88 in.	0	0	0K	0K
2 Varina Grove	06/08/2007	21:45 PM	Thunderstorm Wind	52 kts.	0	0	0K	0K
3 Varina Grove	06/11/2007	14:42 PM	Hail	0.88 in.	0	0	0K	0K
4 Lewis Gardens	06/27/2007	17:35 PM	Thunderstorm Wind	50 kts.	0	0	5K	0K
5 Highland Spgs	07/19/2007	14:45 PM	Thunderstorm Wind	50 kts.	0	0	1K	0K
6 Lewis Gardens	07/19/2007	14:50 PM	Thunderstorm Wind	50 kts.	0	0	1K	0K
7 Lewis Gardens	07/19/2007	14:55 PM	Thunderstorm Wind	50 kts.	0	0	2K	0K
8 Glen Allen	07/29/2007	14:30 PM	Hail	0.75 in.	0	0	0K	0K
9 West End Manor	08/16/2007	18:30 PM	Thunderstorm Wind	50 kts.	0	0	1K	0K
10 Glen Allen	08/16/2007	18:43 PM	Thunderstorm Wind	50 kts.	0	0	1K	0K
11 Quioccasin	08/16/2007	19:00 PM	Thunderstorm Wind	50 kts.	0	0	1K	0K
12 Yellow Tavern	08/16/2007	19:00 PM	Thunderstorm Wind	50 kts.	0	0	1K	0K
13 Yellow Tavern	08/16/2007	21:00 PM	Thunderstorm Wind	50 kts.	0	0	1K	0K
14 Varina Grove	08/16/2007	22:19 PM	Thunderstorm Wind	50 kts.	0	0	1K	0K
15 White Oak Swamp	08/17/2007	12:30 AM	Flash Flood	N/A	0	0	0K	0K
16 Quioccasin	08/19/2007	22:15 PM	Thunderstorm Wind	50 kts.	0	0	1K	0K
17 Dumbarton	08/19/2007	22:40 PM	Thunderstorm Wind	50 kts.	0	0	1K	0K
18 Glen Allen	08/21/2007	16:55 PM	Thunderstorm Wind	50 kts.	0	0	1K	0K
19 Varina Grove	08/21/2007	17:27 PM	Thunderstorm Wind	50 kts.	0	0	1K	0K
20 Richmond Hgts	10/24/2007	12:00 PM	Heavy Rain	N/A	0	0	0K	0K
				TOTALS:	0	0	19K	0

Mag: Magnitude; Dth: Deaths; Inj: Injuries; PrD: Property Damage; CrD: Crop Damage.

The Department of the Interior protects and manages the nation's natural resources and cultural heritage; provides scientific and other information about those resources; and honors its special responsibilities to American Indians, Alaska Natives, and affiliated Island Communities.

NPS 325/102304, 367/102304, May 2010